THE LEGACY OF

ALBERT KAHN

THE LEGACY OF ALBERT KAHN

By W. Hawkins Ferry

With an essay by Walter B. Sanders

Wayne State University Press, Detroit

Library of Congress Cataloging-in-Publication Data

Kahn, Albert, 1869-1942.
    The legacy of Albert Kahn.

    Reprint. Originally published: Detroit: Detroit
Institute of Arts, 1970.
    1. Kahn, Albert, 1869-1942—Exhibitions.
2. Architecture, Modern—19th century—United States—
Exhibitions. 3. Architecture, Modern—20th century—
United States—Exhibitions. I. Ferry, W. Hawkins.
II. Title.
NA737.K28A4 1987   720'.92'4   87-13295
ISBN 0-8143-1888-6
ISBN 0-8143-1889-4 (pbk.)

FRONT COVER
Fisher Building, Detroit, Michigan, 1927
Photo: Hedrich-Blessing

FRONTISPIECE
Albert Kahn, 1940

DESIGNED BY WILLIAM A. BOSTICK

Contents

Sketch of The Arch of Constantine in Rome by Albert Kahn, 1926

Foreword

THE CREATIVE GENIUS of Albert Kahn was celebrated in an exhibition of photographs, drawings, and models of his wide-ranging architectural projects held at the Detroit Institute of Arts from September 15 to November 1, 1970. The first edition of *The Legacy of Albert Kahn* was published as a catalogue to accompany that exhibition. It is a pleasure to see it reissued as part of the Great Lakes Books series of the Wayne State University Press in conjunction with the observance of Michigan's sesquicentennial.

While Albert Kahn's name is firmly established as a major American architect who made important contributions to industrial architecture of the early twentieth century, his buildings also constitute an essential part of the urban fabric of southeastern Michigan. The General Motors and Fisher Buildings as well as the Belle Isle Conservatory and Casino in Detroit, Hill Auditorium and numerous other buildings at the University of Michigan, and many of Michigan's most distinguished private residences exemplify the diversity of his accomplishment.

I would like to thank W. Hawkins Ferry for his renewed support of this volume. He compiled the illustrations, wrote the informative essay, and has generously contributed toward its publication in this edition.

SAMUEL SACHS II
Director, The Detroit Institute of Arts

ALBERT KAHN
1869-1942

by W. Hawkins Ferry

THE CELEBRATION of the seventy-fifth anniversary of Albert Kahn Associates focuses attention upon the modest man who for forty-five years was the driving force of the firm. The bearer of one of the great names in the history of American architecture, the late Albert Kahn is known principally for the contribution he made to the development of modern industrial architecture. What is not so well known is the scope of his work in commercial, civic, institutional and domestic architecture. There are some that begrudge his predilection for historical styles, but few would deny that he brought to each building that he created a searching intelligence and a cool and seasoned aesthetic judgment. If he shared with the architects of his generation a taste for eclecticism, he outdistanced them; for his study of the past gave him the wisdom to give form to the world of the future, and the concepts he developed provided not only the basis for the continuing evolution of his own firm after his death but also an inspiration for a whole new generation of architects.

The story has often been told of Kahn's early struggle to become established in his profession. He was born in 1869 in Rhaunen, Germany, the oldest of six children. His childhood was spent in the Grand Duchy of Luxembourg, where he attended school. His father, Joseph, a rabbi and teacher by profession, believed he might find better opportunities to support his growing family in the New World. The presence of relatives in Detroit prompted him to take his family there in 1880. Success was not as easy to attain as he had hoped, and he and his wife took any odd jobs they could find to make ends meet.

Although early in life young Albert had evinced musical talent, poverty had prevented him from making much headway in this direction. He then dreamed of becoming an artist. In Detroit he found a job in the office of the architect John Scott, but in time he became discouraged at his lack of progress. Hearing of his plight, the sculptor Julius Melchers permitted him to attend his Sunday morning drawing classes free of charge. The discovery that the young pupil was partially color-blind precluded the possibility of becoming an artist, so Melchers found a place for him in the architectural office of Mason and Rice. The pay was small, so Kahn took other small jobs to supplement his parents' meager earnings, for there were now eight children in the family.

Beginning in 1885 as an office boy under George D. Mason, Kahn soon became a draughtsman, learning much about architecture in the firm's excellent library. One of the firm's projects which he worked on was the Gilbert Lee house, which was built on John R Street at Ferry Avenue in Detroit in 1888. In later years the author asked him if he was responsible for the Gothic design of the stone carving over the door of the Lee house. "Yes, that's mine," he said. "It looks like a disease, doesn't it?" The house manifested the typical Richardsonian stylistic characteristics of the day. *Fig. 1*

In 1890 Kahn did work on a summer residence for Dexter M. Ferry on a farm near Unadilla, New York. This involved remodeling and enlarging an old stone farmhouse. In order to emphasize the rich texture of the fieldstone walls, he kept the architectural treatment simple. Projecting and recessed porches made excellent vantage points from which to enjoy the view of the distant hills, and unusual depressed dormer windows broke the roof line and gave the house a snug appearance. The farmer's lodge and the horse barn on the Ferry farm are good examples of the so-called "shingle style" and are interesting studies of masses and textures. *Fig. 2* *Figs. 3, 4*

In 1891 Kahn won a scholarship award of the *American Architect* for a year's study abroad. In Florence he met the architect Henry Bacon, who was later the architect of the Lincoln Memorial in Washington. Bacon was also on a scholarship, and joining together, the two of them wandered from city to city sketching old buildings and architectural details of interest in Italy, France, Belgium, and Germany. Kahn learned a great deal from Bacon. A new world of beauty opened up for him, which he recorded with a fresh spontaneity combined with an accurate sense of form and proportion.

Kahn brought back to Detroit a new vocabulary of design. The William Livingstone house of 1893 on Elliott Street spoke eloquently of his tour of the Loire valley with its elegant French Renaissance details, and the Watson M. Freer house of 1895 on Ferry Avenue made known with its Italian Renaissance details his admiration for the work of Alberti and Bramante. His old mentor, Julius Melchers, had obliged him by translating his designs for ornamental details into stone. *Fig. 5* *Fig. 6*

Kahn's European experience was particularly valuable when Mason and Rice were called upon to design the offices for Hiram Walker and Sons in Windsor, Ontario (1894). The details of the exterior were derived from the sixteenth century Palazzo Pandolfini in Florence. Sketches Kahn had done in Venice and Orleans provided inspiration for the fireplaces and paneling in the lavish individual executive offices, and sketches he had done in Nuremberg gave him ideas for the details in the dark, cozy Sample Room, that inner sanctum of the establishment. *Fig. 7*

In 1896 Kahn left Mason and Rice and joined George W. Nettleton and Alexander B. Trowbridge, who had also been employed in the same office to form the firm of Nettleton, Kahn, and Trowbridge. One of their first jobs was the original building of Children's Hospital on St. Antoine Street in Detroit, which was financed by Hiram Walker (1896). It was obviously not the moment to flaunt the glories of the Italian Renaissance, and the architects produced a simple, practical building with ample fenestration and round bay windows. The treatment of the gables and dormers was Richardsonian, and only the classical entrance reminded one of Kahn's recent pilgrimage to Europe. *Fig. 8*

In 1897 Trowbridge left to become the dean of the Cornell University College of Architecture, and Kahn then worked with Nettleton under the firm name of

Nettleton and Kahn. In 1898 they built the Grace Hospital Nurse's Home on John R Street in the English Jacobean style.

Kahn's feeling of independence and self-confidence was at this time reflected in his personal as well as his professional life, for in 1896 he married Ernestine Krolik, the daughter of a successful drygoods merchant. Soon he was to begin raising a family.

In 1891 Mason and Rice had built a turreted Tudor mansion for James E. Scripps, the president of the *Detroit News,* on Trumbull Avenue in Detroit. A scholarly man, Scripps devoted much of his time to artistic and literary pursuits.

Figs. 9, 10, 11

In 1898 he employed Nettleton and Kahn to build a library and art gallery adjoining his house. The Flemish Renaissance gable end above the entrance of the art gallery prepared one for the works by Dutch and Flemish masters inside, while

Fig. 12

a painstakingly accurate reconstruction of the Chapter House of Westminster Abbey served as a repository for his collection of rare literary treasures. After Scripps' death the building was moved across Trumbull Avenue and joined to the former George Booth house as part of the Scripps Branch Library. The entire complex was demolished in 1967.

When George Nettleton died in 1900, Kahn joined forces again briefly with

Fig. 13

George D. Mason, who had since separated from Rice. They built the Palms Apartment House on Jefferson Avenue in Detroit in 1901-2. This six-story limestone building with Jacobean influence gave Kahn his first opportunity to experiment with reinforced concrete, which was then in a rudimentary stage of development.

Kahn became independent of Mason in 1902. In the following year he

Figs. 14, 15, 16

completed the Temple Beth El on Woodward Avenue. Set well back from the street, the building recalls the Pantheon in Rome, but the decorative treatment is Louis XVI. Kahn's early interest in engineering problems is illustrated by his use of steel trusses supporting the dome. Altered beyond recognition, the building is

Fig. 17

now the Bonstelle Theatre.

The same year that Kahn built the Temple Beth El, he completed the

Fig. 18

Conservatory in Belle Isle Park. Again we find him preoccupied with domical structure, this time in a playful mood. At the same time he built the Aquarium behind the Conservatory. A notable feature of this building is the charming rusticated baroque doorway surmounted by a pediment containing carved dolphins. Both buildings have been modernized in recent years. In 1908 he built

Fig. 19

the Casino on Belle Isle in the Italian Renaissance style. It is a buff-colored brick building with a red tile roof. Surrounding it is a two-story arcaded veranda with corner towers. The second floor veranda opening off the dining room was closed in recently in a rather awkward manner.

The eldest son in the family, Kahn made certain that his brothers' education was more complete than his. Julius, the closest to him in age, was educated in the Detroit public schools and received a B.S. and C.E. degree at the University of Michigan. From 1896 to 1900 he was an engineer for the U.S. Navy and later for the U.S. Engineering Corps. In 1900 he went to Japan to be chief engineer of a group of iron and sulphur mines. Returning to Detroit in 1903, he became associated with his brother Albert as chief engineer.

Fig. 20

They built the Engineering Building at the University of Michigan in Ann Arbor in 1903, using concrete construction. This experience made Julius aware of the weakness of the empirical system of reinforcement. After making conclusive tests, he designed a system of reinforcement based on scientific principles. The U.S. government then made a contract with him to use his form of reinforcement for the War College in Washington. In order to manufacture the so-called Kahn bar, he established the Trussed Concrete Steel Company, of which he became the president. Located in Youngstown, Ohio, it was later called the Truscon Steel Co. until it was absorbed by the Republic Steel Company of Cleveland.

The first industrial building that can definitely be attributed to Albert Kahn was the Boyer Machine Company, which he built for Joseph Boyer on Second Avenue in Detroit in 1901. Soon thereafter the company was merged into the Chicago Pneumatic Tool Company. In 1905 Joseph Boyer employed Kahn to build a factory for the Burroughs Adding Machine Company, of which he was president. Located next to the Chicago Pneumatic Tool Company on Second Avenue, it was a one-story building of conventional iron and wood construction with a saw-tooth roof to provide daylight. The two-story administration building on Second Avenue was entered through a Greek temple-front entrance somewhat similar to the entrance of the Temple Beth El. A newspaper of the day noted that the management of the factory "instead of marring the district in which it is located, has done much to beautify it by the construction of artistic buildings and the improvement of neighboring thoroughfares."

In 1903 Kahn was commissioned to build a new plant for the Packard Motor Car Company on East Grand Boulevard by its President, Henry B. Joy. The two-story building was in the form of a hollow square with windows on all eight sides. The manufacturing processes were arranged to proceed progressively around the square. A contemporary magazine praised the "bright, cleanly, and cheerful aspect of the different departments. It is one of the new style of factories," it noted, "that are gradually displacing the old prison workshops, which, especially in cities, and sadly enough, were common in all industries until the last decade. It is most fitting that the automobile industry as the newest great industry of the country should in its new factories add to the strength of the movement toward rational working places." *Fig. 21*

The first nine buildings of the Packard plant were of conventional mill construction. However, the necessarily restricted distance between columns was objectionable for automobile production, and wood floors soaked with oil were a heavy fire risk in spite of sprinkler systems. Kahn realized that the system of reinforced concrete that his brother had perfected was precisely what was needed to eliminate these shortcomings and he utilized it in the design of building No. 10 of the Packard plant (1905). It was the first factory building of reinforced concrete *Figs. 22, 23, 24*
construction in Detroit. It was originally two stories high, but two more stories were added later. The "Kahn" system soon became established and popular throughout the country.

When the burgeoning automobile industry in Detroit created a demand for more factories, Kahn rose to the occasion. Heretofore architects had considered factory design beneath them, and the task had been relegated to junior draughtsmen. Kahn felt no such compunction. The practical problems encountered appealed to his logical mind. Reconciling himself to the economic necessity of eliminating historical ornament in industrial architecture, he found aesthetic values in the forms engendered by new techniques and functional considerations.

The automobile industry had created a new spirit, and manufacturers were demanding efficient, well lighted and attractive plants. Kahn was able to accommodate them.

Fig. 25

The Grabowsky Power Wagon Company Plant, built about 1907 in Detroit, was an early example of unadorned, straightforward structural expression. It was an expansion of the design of building No. 10 of the Packard plant with wider transverse bays. Four similar parallel units were incorporated in the design of the

Fig. 26

Chalmers Motor Car Company Plant of 1907 on East Jefferson Avenue. These were linked together to form open and closed courts. Broad front lawns dotted with shrubbery and flower beds presented a park-like appearance. An early description of the plant called it "a pleasant place to work." Greatly enlarged, it is now the Chrysler Assembly Plant.

Fig. 27

In 1907 Kahn built the Mergenthaler Linotype Company Plant in Brooklyn, New York. This building was entirely constructed of concrete with no brick wall panels. The wall surface, except at the corners, was reduced to a minimum, and steel sash with opening ventilators were introduced from floor to ceiling.

At about this time Henry Ford was looming on the horizon of the Detroit industrial scene. Like Henry B. Joy, he was constantly looking for ways of improving the efficiency of production. Realizing that his two plants in Detroit were inadequate, he purchased a sixty acre tract in suburban Highland Park with the hope of enlarging and consolidating his operations. He conceived the idea of having an entire plant under one roof with no open courts and no dividing walls, and to make his idea a reality, he sought the assistance of Albert Kahn.

Fig. 28
Fig. 29
Fig. 30

Production began at the Ford Highland Park plant on New Year's day of 1910. Fronting on Woodward Avenue was the four-story concrete main building 840 feet long and 140 feet in breadth. Concrete-slab girder-beam construction was prevalent throughout. For the first time industrial steel sash, which had been imported from England, was used in combination with the concrete frame. In order to relieve the monotony of the building Kahn added brick corner bastions and a cornice, vestiges of traditional architecture which were to disappear in his

Fig. 31

later factories. Parallel to the main building and behind it was the one-story machine shop with a saw-tooth roof. Both these buildings opened upon a crane-

Fig. 32

way, which was between them. The automobile storage area was of steel construction with a skylight running the full length of the building. At the rear was the huge foundry. In front of the main building was the power house with its

Fig. 33

five dramatic smokestacks. Next to this stood the office building, which was of concrete construction. Because of its prominent location, it received more formal architectural treatment than the main building. Beneath the cornice there was a frieze of glazed tiles, and ornamental ironwork screened the second story windows.

In 1912-1915 the continuously moving assembly line was perfected at the

Fig. 34

Highland Park plant. A mock-up of the body assembly line put up outside the plant is shown in the accompanying illustration.

In the meantime plant expansion proceeded apace until the whole complex covered 180 acres. A building of steel construction erected in 1913 illustrates the

Fig. 35

introduction of a continuous monitor extending from one end of the building to

Fig. 36

the other. In 1918 a six-story building of concrete construction with mushroom columns was erected at the rear of the property. Between the units of the building

Fig. 37

were glass-covered courts, which were entered by railroad sidings. There were no sidewalls to the various units. By means of an overhead traveling crane, material was conveyed between the railroad cars to or from the various floor levels. This was facilitated by cantilevered balconies. A comparison may be made here to similar balconies employed in 1926 by Walter Gropius in his design of the Bauhaus at Dessau, Germany.

In 1910 Kahn built the Hudson Motor Car Company on East Jefferson Avenue. It was a large, rectangular three-story building of concrete construction with mushroom columns. Inner courts for light and air reappeared, indicating that Kahn was not prepared to discard them after his experience at Highland Park. In front of the plant was a two-story office building of concrete construction faced *Fig. 38* with stucco. Green tiles were used to frame the entrance and as decorative inserts. An attempt had been made to evolve a simple new architecture expressive of the concrete frame.

Adjacent to the Hudson plant on East Jefferson Avenue, the Continental *Fig. 39* Motor Company plant of 1912 was of steel construction. A saw-tooth roof with *Fig. 40* skylights provided an even distribution of natural light.

In 1910 John F. and Horace E. Dodge, who had supplied automotive engines and parts to Henry Ford, employed Kahn to build a new plant for them on Joseph *Fig. 41* Campau Street in Hamtramck. Three years later they forsook the Ford business, expanded the plant to make cars of their own, and produced the first Dodge automobile in 1914. After the death of both brothers in 1920, the Dodge properties were acquired by the Chrysler Corporation. The original Dodge brothers plant was a four-story concrete complex with inner courts. Some of the larger *Fig. 42* buildings were of steel construction. *Fig. 43*

Later additions to the Burroughs Adding Machine Company (1912-1919) *Fig. 44* consisted of five-story concrete structures with open courts. The same type of construction was utilized in the design of the six-story Fisher Body plant of 1921 *Fig. 45* in Cleveland, Ohio, but the building was flattened out into a long slab-like form, and the vast expanse of wall surface is a particularly handsome example of straightforward, unadorned structural expression.

A photograph taken in 1919 of the interior of the Buick Motor Car Company *Fig. 46* plant in Flint, Michigan, reveals an increasing lightness and openness of the steel frame. The Forge Building of 1910 at the Packard plant in Detroit exhibited *Figs. 47, 48* dramatic new architectural forms expressive of function. Already apparent were the fluid treatment of glass areas and the jagged roof outlines that were to become characteristic earmarks of Kahn factories.

His commercial architecture of this period, although less impressive and more self-conscious than his factories, commands attention for its simplicity and excellence of design. The raw concrete and steel of the industrial work have retreated behind a veneer of brick and glazed terra cotta. "So long as the lines of the building indicate that there is behind them a sustaining skeleton," said Kahn, "and so long as they do not mask the reality and pretend to be the sustaining material, there is no offense."

The Trussed Concrete Building of 1907 was the first office building of con- *Fig. 49* crete construction in Detroit. Located on the northeast corner of Lafayette Boulevard and Wayne Street, it was an eight-story structure with white brick piers, metal spandrels, and a large cornice supported on paired brackets. Later known as the Owen Building, it was torn down in 1957 to make way for the widening of Wayne Street, which is now an extension of Washington Boulevard. The offices of Albert and Julius Kahn were located here in the early years of their careers.

Fig. 50

Figs. 51, 52

Glazed terra cotta was becoming popular as a sheathing for commercial buildings. It provided smooth surfaces and ornamental detail at a fraction of the cost of stone. Kahn used this material on the facade of the Grinnell Brothers Building of 1908 on Woodward Avenue. Walls were reduced to a minimum, and spandrels and mullions were fabricated of iron. The National Theatre of 1910 on Monroe Street gave Kahn an opportunity for an imaginative use of terra cotta in a theatrical neo-baroque design, greatly enhanced by night illumination. This theatre, once devoted to vaudeville and motion pictures, is now a burlesque house.

Fig. 53

The Palmer Office and Store Building (1910), now the Robinson Furniture Company, on Washington Boulevard approached the Sullivanian ideal. Here the wall surface was reduced to a terra cotta grille expressing the concrete frame. In 1909-10 Chicago architect Daniel Burnham built two skyscrapers in Detroit, the Ford Building and the Dime Building on Griswold Street. That Kahn was influenced by the work of the great Chicagoan is apparent in his design of the

Figs. 54, 55, 56

Ford Motor Company Service Building, later called the Boulevard Building, which he built in 1913 at the intersection of Woodward Avenue and Grand Boulevard. Here ornament was reduced to a minimum, and the overall design, in its simplicity and clarity, came the closest to Kahn's industrial work of any of his commercial buildings. Unfortunately, the Boulevard Building has recently been drastically altered by the removal of the terra cotta veneer and the substitution of horizontal bands of stone veneer.

For buildings over eight stories high, concrete construction was not only impractical but uneconomical. Kahn utilized a steel frame for the ten-story Detroit

Fig. 57

Free Press Building of 1913 on Lafayette Boulevard (now the Transportation Building). The street facade was faced with ornate terra cotta. His tallest building

Fig. 58

of the period was the eighteen-story Kresge Building of 1914 on Grand Circus Park (now the Kales Building). Here the Burnham tradition lingered on. Brick piers combined with terra cotta spandrels terminated in an unusual shallow gable

Fig. 59

with a suppressed cornice. The twelve-story Vinton Building of 1917 (now the American Savings Association) on Woodward Avenue at Congress Street belongs in the same category as the Kresge Building.

Fig. 60

In 1916 Kahn built the A. Krolik and Company Warehouse Building for his father-in-law on East Jefferson Avenue. It was a simple, straightforward building of warm, buff-colored brick. Since there was little need for ornament, it was limited mainly to brickwork patterns around the top of the building. The cornice was completely eliminated.

Fig. 61

The Detroit News Building of 1915 on Lafayette and Second Boulevards was Kahn's most monumental building of the period. According to a contemporary account, George G. Booth, the president of the *Detroit News*, "was determined that the new home of the *News* should possess the dignity of style, chastity of spirit, and substantiality appropriate to an institution which is aware of its intimate association with the welfare of the individual and the state." Kahn found what Booth was looking for in the solid-looking buildings that had given German cities such an air of prosperity before World War I. In the heavy stone arches, piers and mullions of the Detroit News Building there is something of the character of the work of Messel, Olbrich, or Behrens in Germany. "During the past fifty years," wrote Kahn, "there has been a general revival of good taste, keener interest in and appreciation of all the arts. Germany led the van in cutting away from the debased in vogue. In the work of Messel, we see perhaps the first serious abandonment of prevalent tradition and establishment of a new type of work expressive of the modern trend."

Although Kahn's commercial architecture, generally speaking, was somewhat conservative, occasionally it displayed a daring ingenuity that was reminiscent of his industrial work. In his Hudson Motor Car Company display room of 1910 in Detroit, exposed structural steel beams were expressed as a decorative element.
Fig. 62

In 1912 Kahn went on a vacation trip to Italy. As on his previous trip, he carried his sketch pad with him and recorded buildings and architectural details of interest. In Siena and Bologna, he sketched the old palaces and churches with their mellow brickwork studded with terra cotta insets. On the margin of the sketches he made detailed annotations of the size and placement of the bricks. This experience was useful to him when he returned to Detroit. Relying for surface treatment upon the rich patina of brick enlivened with terra cotta, he designed a series of buildings at the University of Michigan in Ann Arbor that blended with the informal landscaped setting.

The sombre dignity of the collonaded stone entrance of the Hill Auditorium (1913), somewhat reminiscent of the design of the Detroit News Building, is relieved by the informality of the rest of the building with its rich surface brickwork. The window treatment on the side of the building is closely related to the work of Louis Sullivan. Also somewhat Sullivanian is the round arch above the stage on the interior. The plan is parabolic with the speaker's stand at the focal point to assure the best acoustics.
Fig. 63

Fig. 64
Figs. 65, 66

Fig. 67

There is a parallel between the Natural Science Building (1917) and Kahn's industrial work. The concrete frame permitted a reduction of wall surface and an increase in window area. However, the careful detailing of brick, terra cotta, and stone gave the building an academic rather than an industrial appearance. The plan is a hollow square with an auditorium placed diagonally at the corner. Continuing in the same vein, the General Library (1919) achieved a monumental dignity without resorting to a classical portico or a grand staircase.
Figs. 68, 69

Fig. 70

Fig. 71

Fig. 72

During World War I Kahn designed the majority of army airfields and many naval bases for the United States government. The Laboratory Building of the U.S. Aviation School at Langley Field, Virginia (1917), was subtly designed with broad eaves and slender piers between the windows. The fine brickwork of the building was enlivened with attractive tile patterns. Even the hangar at Langley Field was embellished with tiles.
Fig. 73
Figs. 74, 75
Fig. 76

The Grosse Pointe Shores Village Hall near Detroit (1915) belongs to the above group of highly original brick buildings but is on a smaller almost domestic scale.
Fig. 77

It was natural that Kahn should have turned to England for inspiration for his domestic architecture, since it was there that the greatest progress had been made in this field. Turning their backs on the artificial pretensions of Victorian architecture, the English architects had rediscovered the charm and livability of the traditional English dwelling. The importance of the plan was emphasized, and the principle was re-established of basing the plan on the organized life of the building. Closely allied with the revival of domestic architecture in England was the arts and crafts movement, which championed a reform in the decorative arts. The movement spread to America, and one of the most active organizations founded to further the cause was the Detroit Society of Arts and Crafts. Kahn became a founding craftsman of the Society in 1906 and maintained a lifelong interest in its activities.

In the early part of his career, Kahn's domestic work was extensive, but, as he became more involved in industrial architecture, he only had time to design a few houses as special favors to his major clients. He leaned toward either Tudor or Georgian design but was never slavishly imitative. He considered it important to adapt his houses to the requirements of modern living. It was also important to relate each house to its grounds and to make sure that the most important rooms were on the opposite side of the house from the formal entrance and that they opened upon inviting terraces, gardens, and lawns.

Figs. 78, 79
One of Kahn's important early residential commissions was the Charles M. Swift house on East Jefferson Avenue in Grosse Pointe (1903). It is a gray stone *Figs. 80, 81, 82* Tudor house with a gray slate roof facing Lake St. Clair. In 1905 Kahn built an imposing Tudor mansion for E. Chandler Walker in Windsor, Ontario. The epitome of Edwardian elegance, it combined stone walls and half-timbered wall areas *Fig. 83* under a grouping of picturesque medieval roofs and chimneys. In the center of the house a large manorial hall opened on a series of impressive rooms. The house is now the Art Gallery of Windsor.

Figs. 84, 85
An architect's own house is always very revealing, for it illustrates the kind of architecture he personally prefers. The Kahn house of 1907 on Mack Avenue at John R Street in Detroit was a distinct departure from the ostentatious and archeological Tudor style of the Walker house. It followed rather the simplified style of the second generation of architects of the Domestic Revival in England. The medieval prototype was abstracted. Windows were grouped wherever needed, and materials were used for their own aesthetic value rather than for their *Figs. 86, 87, 88* antiquarian connotations. The interior woodwork and furnishings reflected Kahn's taste for craftsmanship, which had been nurtured by his European travels and reinforced by his affiliation with the arts and crafts movement. Most of the furniture he designed himself. Behind the house was an extensive garden. "The garden is more important than the house to me," said Kahn. "I like to play at landscape gardening," he continued. "I believe as much should be spent for land as for the house in cities." In 1928, he added a gallery to his house, which will be described later. The house is now the headquarters of the Urban League.

Figs. 89, 90, 91, 92
In 1907 Kahn built a house for George G. Booth, the president of the *Detroit News*, on a large estate in Bloomfield Hills. It is understandable that Booth, as president of the Arts and Crafts Society, should have been in sympathy with Kahn's new trend toward simplicity. The house was on a much grander scale than Kahn's own home, but the same restraint in design and materials prevailed. A decade later two wings were added on each side of the forecourt. The west wing contained the library and the east wing the Oak Room. Paneled wood in both rooms was carved by John Kirchmayer, a native of Oberammergau. Terraces around the house overlooked extensive landscaped gardens and a small artificial lake.

Fig. 93
Fig. 94
The William L. Clements house of 1908 in Bay City, Michigan, was somewhat similar to the Booth house. The two-story library with a beamed ceiling and

a balcony was a particularly charming and inviting room. Later, Kahn was to build the William L. Clements Library of American History at the University of Michigan.

Horace E. Dodge was a different type of man from George Booth or William L. Clements. A house in the so-called "cottage style" favored by these men would not have appealed to him. He was an energetic man who had made a fortune through his own efforts and demanded a more vigorous, assertive style of architecture for his domicile. The house that rose on the shores of Lake St. Clair in Grosse Pointe in 1910 was a gabled Jacobean house of rugged red sandstone with a green tile roof. The interior was notable for its handsome paneling and elaborate wood carving. "Rose Terrace," as the place was called, was demolished after Mr. Dodge's death, and a new "Rose Terrace" in the style of Louis XV was built by Horace Trumbauer for Mrs. Dodge. *Figs. 95, 96* *Figs. 97, 98 ,99*

Kahn returned to the cottage style in his design of the rambling Detroit Golf Club of 1916 on Hamilton Road in Detroit. The fine brickwork, interesting roof masses and broad verandas make this a building of great charm and originality. *Figs. 100, 101, 102*

While the organic quality of the cottage style appealed to Kahn, he was also attracted by the discipline and regularity of Renaissance architecture. He used the Georgian colonial idiom in his design of the red brick Country Club of Detroit on Lake Shore Road in Grosse Pointe (1905). The cardinal features of the design were the hipped roofs repeated in the smaller hipped roofs of the dormers and the vast projecting verandas designed to catch the breezes from Lake St. Clair. The building was demolished when a new country club was built near the golf course in 1926. *Figs. 103, 104*

The same style of architecture was used in the design of the Henry B. Joy residence on Lake Shore Road in Grosse Pointe (1908). Mr. Joy, the President of the Packard Motor Car Company, was a practical man, who had no desire for architectural histrionics. He enjoyed yachting, and his yacht was moored to a dock projecting into Lake St. Clair in front of his house. The dining room, living room, and sun room of the house formed a long continuous area exposed to the lake view by means of large windows at regular intervals. Here the uncompromising rationality of Kahn's industrial work was applied to his domestic architecture, and a certain similarity may be noted between Joy's residence and his Packard plant. The floors were of concrete construction, but brick walls and a hipped roof provided a domestic character. The house was torn down in 1958 and the property subdivided. *Fig. 105* *Fig. 106*

In the early years of the twentieth century, Charles A. Platt, the New York architect, had introduced to the American architectural scene the restrained elegance and easy refinement of the Italian villa. He had found in Italy that the villa and the garden are designed as a unit for the enjoyment of the owner. In view of Kahn's interest in landscape architecture, it is not surprising that he greatly admired the work of Platt. When Russell A. Alger, Jr., was considering building a mansion in Grosse Pointe, Kahn, with self-effacing modesty, recommended Platt as the architect. Completed in 1910 "The Moorings," as the Alger house was called, set a new standard of elegance in Grosse Pointe.

The initial impact of the work of Platt upon Kahn is apparent in the design of the Lake Shore Road residence of Philip McMillan, a Director of the Packard Motor Car Company (1912). Classical proportions and details were emphasized, *Figs. 107, 108* white stucco walls were combined with a red tile roof, and French doors were introduced opening on a broad terrace overlooking a lawn sloping toward the lake. By 1915, Kahn had created a full-blown Italian villa in the Platt tradition for Goodloe Edgar on Lake Shore Road. A balustrated terrace flanked by two loggias commanded a magnificent panorama of the lake, and at the side of the house was a formal garden.

Fig. 109

In 1915 Kahn built a house on Lake Shore Road for John S. Newberry, one of the founders of the Packard Motor Car Company and the son and namesake of one of Detroit's most prominent industrialists of the nineteenth century. Ernest Wilby, an associate of Kahn, who designed the house, appears to have been influenced by the work of Platt. Like Platt, he emphasized noble proportions, restrained elegance, and fine details and was able to blend diverse styles subtly without any apparent discrepancy. Although the white stucco walls and red tile roof associated with the Italian villa were retained, the exterior proportions and some details of the Newberry house were French, while the windows were English.

Figs. 110, 111

Fig. 112

The interior was a masterpiece of formal planning with exquisite details. The main hall was a vast Jacobean room paneled in curled maple (?) and containing a magnificent staircase with a carved balustrade and newel posts. To the east was the Georgian dining room paneled in walnut with carving in the manner of Grinling Gibbons, and to the west was the living room containing an impressive Italian Renaissance fireplace. Parquet floors in the principal rooms were of teak. A veranda on the east side of the house faced a formal garden. To the north French doors opened upon a terrace which overlooked extensive lawns and gardens. After World War II, increasing taxes and a scarcity of domestic employees made the survival of the great mansions of Grosse Pointe precarious. After the death of Mrs. Newberry in 1956 the house was torn down and the property subdivided.

Fig. 113
Fig. 114
Fig. 115
Fig. 116
Figs. 117, 118
Fig. 119
Fig. 120

More modest in scale than the Newberry house was the Frank and Robert Kuhn house of 1914 on McKinley Road in Grosse Pointe. Here Kahn returned to the essential simplicity of the colonial tradition. A continuing interest in brickwork may be noted in the unconventional use of tapestry brick, which provided an interesting textural quality. Kahn built the house as a favor to the Kuhn brothers because he had built their factory in Detroit.

Fig. 121

The cottage style and the colonial tradition were freely blended in the design of the Frank L. Klingensmith house of 1916. Situated in the rolling countryside of Bloomfield Hills, this white stucco house with a red tile roof was surrounded by formal gardens divided by low fieldstone walls. Klingensmith was the Vicepresident, Treasurer, and a Director of the Ford Motor Company.

Figs. 122, 123

The most modern dwelling that Kahn ever produced was his summer cottage on Walnut Lake in Oakland County near Detroit (1917). Here he could relax freed from the pressures of city life. There was no need for historical reference in the design of the simple frame building. Its low, horizontal lines related it to the domestic architecture of the Prairie School of Chicago. Continuous bands of casement windows caught the summer breezes, and screened porches provided a link with the out-of-doors. Near the house was a garden, beyond which the ground sloped abruptly toward the lake.

Figs. 124, 125

Fig. 126

The cottage at Walnut Lake might have been the beginning of an entirely new departure in Kahn's work, but the taste of his clients and his own reverence for the past led him increasingly toward more traditional forms in his nonindustrial work. "If, in re-employing older forms and applying them to our newer problems, we have done wrong," he declared, "then all architecture of the past is wrong, for all of it is but a development of what was done before."

During this period he turned to New York rather than to Chicago for inspiration. Charles A. Platt had brought some of the magic he found in the Italian villa to the suburbs of New York, while McKim, Mead, and White had borrowed freely from classical antiquity and the Italian Renaissance to provide New York itself with an elegance commensurate with its increasing importance as a world metropolis. Referring to Charles F. McKim of the firm of McKim, Mead, and White, Kahn observed, "I have little patience with those who claim his work archeology and not architecture. Indeed, he found his inspiration in the past, but he knew how to employ the best of the old to do service to the new. His was never slavish copyism but a judicious adaptation of established forms with plenty of his own individuality incorporated. He was an artist in the finest sense of the word."

Drawing their inspiration from the Italian palace, McKim, Mead, and White built several elegant men's clubs in New York at the turn of the century. This followed a precedent established by Sir Charles Barry in London a century before. Kahn continued the tradition in his design for the Detroit Athletic Club of 1915. *Figs. 127, 128* Many of the details were based on sketches he had made of palaces in Rome and Florence on a trip to Italy in 1912.

Italian Renaissance and classical details lent dignity and authority to the Police Headquarters Building on Beaubien Street in Detroit (1921). Here Kahn *Fig. 129* blended traditional forms with the pier and spandrel fenestration of his commercial architecture.

Kahn's understanding of functional organization led him inevitably into the field of hospital design. To his credit are Herman Kiefer Hospital and buildings for Harper and Woman's Hospitals in Detroit. His masterpiece was the University Hospital in Ann Arbor (1920). A generous site and the requirement to build the *Fig. 130* entire hospital in one building provided an opportunity for bold and imaginative *Fig. 131* planning. Considering its early date, the hospital is surprisingly modern in concept. The only concession to his contemporaneous interest in traditionalism was the monumental stone administrative unit, which, nevertheless, provided a pleasant contrast to the rather stark functionalism of the remainder of the building.

Ernest Wilby, Kahn's associate from 1903 to 1918, was one of the most talented designers in the Kahn office. He had designed the original Ford Highland Park plant and in a somewhat related style had created the Hill Auditorium and the Natural Science Building at the University of Michigan. He had pioneered in the search for new ways of expressing the concrete frame externally. His departure from the Kahn office coincided with a return to academicism.

The committee in charge of campus development during the twenties at the University of Michigan recommended a combination of modernism and classicism in the design of university buildings. Kahn, who was the supervising architect, followed its suggestion. A typical example was the Medical Building of 1925. Here *Fig. 132* brick was no longer used as an expressive medium, and classicism reappeared in a monumental Ionic order. More imposing in its classic monumentality was the Doric portico of Angell Hall (1922), which was probably inspired by the *Fig. 133* Lincoln Memorial in Washington by Henry Bacon, Kahn's early friend and mentor.

The generosity of William L. Clements enabled Kahn to design the jewel-like

Fig. 134

Clements Library in Ann Arbor to house the Clement collection of rare Americana. It is a one-story limestone structure in the style of the Italian Renaissance with a triple-arched portico flanked by two narrow bays. There is, of course, an obvious parallel to the Morgan Library in New York by McKim, Mead, and White, but actually the building bears a closer resemblance to the same firm's Butler Institute of American Art in Youngstown, Ohio. The design of the latter was derived from a casino by Vignola in the gardens of the Villa Farnese at Caprarola. Kahn admired the original structure in Italy and photographed it on one of his numerous trips abroad.

It is not surprising that Kahn's most monumental building was his second

Fig. 135

Temple Beth El built in 1927 further out Woodward Avenue in Detroit than the first one. The purely classical facade with its imposing portico and temple doorways struck a note of awesome dignity. Although the temple is quite different in concept from the library of Columbia University by McKim, Mead, and White, a similarity may be noted between the Ionic colonnades of both buildings.

The elegance of New York soon permeated Kahn's commercial work. The

Fig. 136

prototype for his Detroit Trust Company of 1915 (now the Detroit Bank and Trust Company) was the Knickerbocker Trust Company by McKim, Mead, and White in New York. A colonnade of Corinthian columns gave the impression of wealth, permanence and security, yet still permitted generous fenestration. On

Fig. 137

the interior marble walls and floors and a gilded coffered ceiling sustained the mood of opulence. In 1926 the building was widened one hundred feet to the west, and in 1966 it was completely modernized.

Fig. 138

In the design of the handsome Packard sales room of 1915 on East Jefferson Avenue in Detroit, classical details were subordinated to practical requirements. The columns having been reduced to pilasters, the building became a glass cage.

Fig. 139

The main sales room of the Ford Motor Company in New York (1917) was a light, airy place not without the elegance afforded by marble columns and a marble grand staircase.

Fig. 140

The twenty-four story National Bank Building in Detroit (1922) continued the skyscraper tradition of Burnham with a greater classical emphasis. Stone veneer took the place of terra cotta, and Corinthian columns similar to those noted on the exterior of the Detroit Trust Company were introduced at the base of the building on the level of the main banking room. A perspective drawing of this

Fig. 141

room by Ivan Dise of the Kahn office gives the impression of Roman magnificence.

Fig. 142

In 1922 Kahn built the enormous General Motors Building on West Grand Boulevard in Detroit. Its success as a design may be attributed to the emphasis upon simple massing rather than detail. Four identical cross-wings jut out like massive promontories to form open courts. The old law of vertical division into base, shaft and cap was followed, but the ornamentation is restrained and well scaled. Crowning the building is a Corinthian colonnade, and at the base is an

Fig. 143
Fig. 144

Italian Renaissance arcade. The triple arched entrance portico is closely related in design to the one at the Clements Library. On the interior marble walls and floors and gilded coffered ceilings strike a note of restrained luxury.

In the late twenties Kahn's commercial work reflected changes that were taking place in architectural concepts in New York, particularly as a result of

Fig. 145

set-back laws. The Free Press Building (1925) and the Maccabees Building (1927) were composed of tower masses supported on lower stories. Cornices disappeared and a vertical accent was effected by emphasizing vertical piers.

Fig. 146

Kahn's greatest opportunity in commercial architecture came when he was commissioned to design the Fisher Building (1927) on West Grand Boulevard in Detroit. It was to be the first and largest of three units of a vast shopping and office complex planned by the Fisher brothers of the Fisher Body Company. This would provide a secondary business district that would relieve the congestion in downtown Detroit and at the same time be more accessible to the suburbs.

Figs. 147, 148

The aesthetic aspects of such an important commission required considerable study. Kahn was alarmed about the trend of architecture in the ebullient twenties. In his opinion Le Corbusier, Gropius, and Mendelsohn had gone too far in the glorification of steel and glass. He recognized that the modern skyscraper deserved an exterior treatment expressive of its structure, but he was wary of indulging in the strange or the bizarre. In an article he wrote about modern architecture in a periodical of the day he stated: "The attempt to continue a vital architecture and one related to and enriching our own time instead of merely repeating old forms is, of course, proper. What is wrong with the movement today is the throwing to the winds all precedent, the idea that new style may be created by an abandonment of all old."

The architect Cass Gilbert of New York had found an analogy between the soaring lines of the skyscraper and those of the Gothic cathedral. He endowed his Woolworth Building and New York Life Insurance Company Building with Gothic details and silhouettes. The latter building with its steep Gothic roof was probably the prototype of the Fisher Building, but Gilbert's fussy Gothic details were abandoned in favor of a more modern decorative treatment. In his design of the Fisher Building, Kahn was undoubtedly also influenced by the work of Holabird and Root in Chicago and of Eliel Saarinen, who was then President of the Cranbrook Academy of Art in Bloomfield Hills, Michigan. The building is basically L-shaped in plan with the 26-story tower at the corner. Shop windows facing the streets on two sides of the building are framed with round arches, and a magnificent marble-walled arcade, giving access to the shops from the rear, extends from one end of the building to the other. Géza Maróti, whom Eliel Saarinen brought to Cranbrook from Hungary, designed the architectural sculpture and the mosaics on the vaults of the arcade.

Fig. 149

The volume of commercial architecture produced by the Kahn office during the thirties was reduced because of the depression; but some interesting pavilions were built at expositions. When Kahn built the Ford Exposition Building at the Chicago World's Fair of 1933, he realized that any historical styles would be meaningless, so he chose the automobile gear as a symbolic form for the building. Later the pavilion was moved to Dearborn to be used as a display room. The Ford Exposition Building at the New York World's Fair cf 1939 included a spiral ramp known as the "Road of Tomorrow," which was continuously traversed by thirty-six bright red, blue, and yellow Fords.

Fig. 150
Fig. 151

While Kahn's commercial and industrial architecture were becoming more modern, his domestic architecture became increasingly archeological. This dichotomy in his work reflected the contrast between the business worlds of his clients and the private worlds to which they retreated. The restless and opulent era of the twenties not only stimulated modernity but it permitted indulgence in the extravagant and theatrical. On one hand architects looked toward the future, and on the other they yearned for the dignity, charm and mellowness of earlier ages. Particularly in the field of domestic architecture, the accent was on the picturesque, and the variety of picturesqueness was a matter of personal choice.

Kahn had always admired the Tudor style, but his attention was now focused on the particular type of Tudor architecture found in the Cotswold district of England. Henry Ford, on one of his numerous trips abroad, was attracted by the rambling informal stone houses of this remote area and had one moved to Greenfield Village, his outdoor museum of historic buildings in Dearborn. Henry's son, Edsel, had visited the Cotswold district with his father and liked the local dwellings so much that, when he and Mrs. Ford asked Kahn to build a house for them in Grosse Pointe, they wanted it to be in the Cotswold style. They studied the style in England, and Kahn went abroad for further study.

Fig. 152   Built in 1926, the Ford house is faced with sandstone. The stones for the roof were imported from England, and expert British workmen were also brought in to split the stones and lay them on the roof in authentic Cotswold manner. The large stone Tudor main hall opens upon a loggia and open terrace toward the lake.

Fig. 153   The principal rooms are distinguished by imported antique carved paneling either
Fig. 154   in the Tudor or Georgian style. Joined to the house by a connecting passage is the huge gallery in the Cotswold style, which has stone walls and oak plank flooring with wood pins. At the end of the gallery is an immense antique stone fireplace imported from England.

Mr. Alvan T. Macauley, the president of the Packard Motor Car Company, and Mrs. Macauley visited England and also became enamored of Cotswold archi-
Figs. 155, 156, 157   tecture. The house which Kahn built for them in 1928 on Lake Shore Road in Grosse Pointe is somewhat similar to the Ford house but is faced with rock faced limestone instead of sandstone ashlar, which gives it a somewhat more informal
Figs. 158, 159   character. The principal rooms are beautifully paneled, but the paneling is not antique. The living room is large and manorial with a beamed ceiling. The house is now owned by Mr. Alfred R. Glancy, Jr.

Fig. 160   In 1928 Kahn built a house on a large estate in Bloomfield Hills for James Couzens, who had been Treasurer and General Manager of the Ford Motor Company and later became the Mayor of Detroit and then a senator from Michigan. The house is a much freer interpretation of the Tudor style than the Ford or Macauley houses. It is built of red brick with a slate roof. The interior is notable for its ornate carved paneling. The estate was recently sold to the Chrysler Corporation and will be subdivided, the house remaining as a club for residents.

The dignity and charm of the Tudor style appealed to Kahn so much that in
Figs. 161, 162, 163   1928 he added a large Tudor gallery to his own house in Detroit. Paneled walls and a moulded plaster ceiling enriched the room, and a mullioned bay window with leaded sash provided a view of the garden. Here he displayed his collection of impressionist paintings, which included works by Degas, Renoir, Monet, Sisley, and Pissarro. At the opposite end of the gallery from the fireplace was a grand
Fig. 164   piano, which afforded him many hours of enjoyment and relaxation. Near the piano was a small table where he played checkers.

For many years Kahn was an Arts Commissioner of the Detroit Institute of Arts. In this position his judgment was invaluable in solving problems, and he gave many carefully selected works of art to the museum to round out the collection. He was instrumental in choosing Paul P. Cret of Philadelphia as architect of the Detroit Institute of Arts (1927). The accompanying photograph shows him at the ground breaking ceremony. The building proved to be a masterpiece of Italian Renaissance architecture.

Fig. 165

The eye that was trained to see beauty in the art and architecture of the past was able to visualize beauty in the design of a factory. In this branch of architecture, economic considerations and a lack of historical precedent precluded traditional concepts and materials. According to Kahn, himself:

"The problems (of plant design) as a rule give scope for constructive thinking and planning, afford opportunity for exercising sound judgment in arrangement and, last but not least, for attractive grouping and external treatment. In regard to the latter, it is proven that a straightforward attack of the problem, the direct solution generally applied, that avoidance of unnecessary ornamentation, simplicity and proper respect for cost of maintenance, make for a type which, though strictly utilitarian and functional, has distinct architectural merit."

After his triumph at Highland Park, Henry Ford was not satisfied to rest on his laurels. Irked by the threat of shortages, high prices and strikes, he envisioned a vast super plant that would be self-sufficient. With this in mind he purchased a vast tract in a desolate area near Detroit where the River Rouge flows into the Detroit River. Rail transportation was adequate, and the River Rouge could be deepened and converted into a harbor.

Developments at River Rouge took an unexpected turn when Ford was assigned the task of manufacturing Eagle boats during World War I. In those days ship building was an outdoor affair, but Ford thought the work would go faster inside. He saw the advantage of utilizing assembly line methods developed at Highland Park. Convinced of the inefficiency of multi-story factories, he envisioned a continuous flow of work on one level. Kahn was able to accommodate him with a half-mile long building with a steel frame and walls that were an unbroken expanse of glass. Building B, as the structure was called, made architectural history. After the war it was converted to the manufacture of automobiles.

Fig. 166

In the twenties the Rouge plant began rapidly expanding until it was soon to become the largest industrial plant in the world. Huge factory buildings sprawled over the vast acreage, connected by a network of railroad tracks. In 1921 Kahn built the main power plant with its eight tall smokestacks, which became a familiar landmark on the horizon. Characteristic examples of the many buildings which followed were the glass plant and open hearth mills of 1924-5. Here clerestories and butterfly roofs were dramatic expressions of functional requirements. The detached smokestacks of the glass plant achieved a monumental quality.

Fig. 167

Fig. 168

Figs. 169, 170

The Ford Engineering Laboratory of 1925 in Dearborn is an exceptional example of the classical influence upon Kahn's industrial architecture. In addition to being a laboratory, it was also the headquarters of the *Ford News,* the *Dearborn Independent* and the Ford radio stations. Its importance in the Ford empire probably accounts for its classical architectural treatment. Considerable care was also taken in the design of the interior of the building, where an abundance of light was provided and where all piping and conduits were concealed in the beams and columns. Even the power house of the laboratory was classical. The same classical influence could be seen in the exterior of the office building of the Hudson Motor

Fig. 171

Fig. 172

Fig. 173

Car Company in Detroit after it was enlarged and remodeled in 1931.

A typical Kahn factory of the twenties is the Plymouth Plant of the Chrysler Corporation (1928) on Lynch Road at Mt. Elliott Avenue in Detroit. The entire factory, one-half mile in length, is on one level and under one roof. Natural lighting is provided by glass curtain walls and various types of monitors.

A Soviet commission visited Detroit and made a tour of automobile factories in 1929. When they found that Albert Kahn was the architect of most of the factories, they asked him to build a tractor plant at Stalingrad. Completed in 1930, the project was so successful that Kahn was requested to aid in the organization of all Russia on an industrial basis. Under the supervision of Mortiz Kahn, the brother of Albert, a force of architects, engineers and superintendents was sent to Russia to teach Russians American industrial practices. In two years they had built 521 factories from Kiev to Yakutsk and trained over a thousand Soviet engineers and apprentices to carry on their work. The Tractor Plant at Chaliabinsk (1933) was an example of their work.

In 1936 Kahn built the Strip Mill for Republic Steel Corporation in Cleveland, Ohio. Up until that time, it was customary for steel companies to employ their own engineers to design their plants because of the specialized knowledge required of production processes. This was the first strip mill in the country to be designed by a firm of independent architects, and a saving of 2,100 tons of steel was effected.

The tire plant at the River Rouge Plant of the Ford Motor Company (1936) is an example of clean-cut, straightforward factory design. Rectangular monitors provide a high quality of natural lighting. In the design of the warehouse of the Kelvinator Corporation (1936) at Plymouth, Michigan, canopied shipping docks and glass curtain walls are dramatically combined. Reaching the ultimate in simplification of form, the Diesel Engine plant of the General Motors Corporation (1937) in Redford Township, Michigan, is merely a rectangular box with walls consisting of brick, clear glass and translucent glass. At the Lady Esther Plant (1938) at Clearing, Illinois, the curtain wall achieves elegance by the elimination of muntins and the careful articulation of units.

Lightweight curtain walls on a vast scale and an extraordinary purity of form have made the De Soto Press Shop of the Chrysler Corporation (1936) a classic of modern architecture. Built in 1936, it is located on Michigan and Wyoming Avenues in Detroit. Referring to this building, architectural critic George Nelson wrote, "Conservatives may rebel at the application of architectural criteria to such structures, but the fact remains that it is precisely in such buildings that modern architecture has reached its most complete expression."

In 1938 the Chrysler Corporation built the Dodge Half-Ton Truck Plant in Warren, Michigan. The administrative offices adjoining the assembly building are handsome in their unadorned simplicity. Of particular interest is the roof structure of the assembly building. The roof is supported on cantilevered bent steel beams, and the monitors hang below the roof level instead of projecting above it, thus improving the natural illumination.

The export building of the Half-Ton Truck Plant, somewhat similar to the De Soto Press Shop, has also received the acclaim of architectural critics and historians. In comparison with the earlier building, there is a greater subtlety in the design of the end wall. The machine shop of the Ohio Steel Foundry Company

(1938) at Lima, Ohio, is similar in design.

An unusual type of monitor may be seen in the manufacturing building of the Glenn L. Martin Company in Baltimore, Maryland (1937). Here pairs of monitors with shed roofs interrupt the roof line, creating an interesting pattern. The uncompromising expression of functionally prescribed form is strikingly relevant to current architecture. The assembly building of the Glenn L. Martin Company was built on a vast scale in anticipation of a future increase in the size of planes. The client required interior space unobstructed by columns. To accommodate him, Kahn built the longest flat-span trusses ever used in a building.

Fig. 196

Fig. 197

Fig. 198
Figs. 199, 200
Fig. 201

The Burroughs Adding Machine Company Plant in Plymouth, Michigan (1938) called for a different architectural treatment from the Glenn Martin Plant, as the product manufactured was small. Kahn returned to the multi-story plant of concrete construction. He had greatly admired buildings by Emil Fahrenkamp and Wilhelm Kreis of Dusseldorf, Germany, and the influence of their work is apparent in the fine brickwork and carefully studied masses of the Burroughs Plant.

Brickwork was used again on the facade of the press shop (1939) at the River Rouge Plant but in this case rather superficially. One of the largest industrial buildings ever erected, the press shop required the largest amount of steel ever used in one building. An elevated level was used for many of the presses, permitting the use of conveyors on the ground level.

Fig. 202
Fig. 203

By 1938 the volume of Kahn's work reached a total of nineteen percent of all architect-designed U.S. industrial building. He had developed a new concept of the architectural office. The departments of technical division designed the entire construction including the mechanical trades. This speeded up the making of drawings, which could be completed in a week or ten days if necessary. The executive division was responsible for the management of the job in the course of construction. With the advent of World War II, Albert Kahn, Incorporated, was called upon to expand in order to help make America the "Arsenal of Democracy." The office staff was increased from 400 to 600, and the day's work was stretched to meet building schedules for war plants.

The Chrysler Tank Arsenal at Warren, Michigan (1941) was the first heavy tank plant in America. With its vast expanse of glass curtain wall, it is reminiscent of Building "B," which Kahn built at the Ford River Rouge Plant during World War I.

Figs. 204, 205

In contrast with the usual unsightly type of foundry construction, the cast armor plant of the American Steel Foundries Company (1941) at East Chicago, Indiana, compares favorably with other types of factories. The curtain walls are composed of three rows of continuous sash separated by strips of asbestos siding, and the ends of the monitors are integrated in the overall design.

Fig. 206

The same type of treatment prevails in the design of the machine shop of the American Locomotive Company (1942) at Auburn, New York, with greater refinement of detail. Stucco and glass curtain walls are combined in a design of great simplicity and purity. The interior is extremely well lighted. Another variation in the same type of exterior treatment but on a more human scale may be seen in the design of the Torpedo Plant of the Amertorp Corporation (1942) in Chicago.

Fig. 207

Fig. 208

Figs. 209, 210

To facilitate the production of airplanes during the war, Kahn was called upon to build many of the principal airplane factories. The Willow Run Bomber Plant of the Ford Motor Company (1943) at Ypsilanti, Michigan, was the largest

Fig. 211

Fig. 211

war plant in the world. Here the B-24 was mass-produced in the same manner as the automobile. Because of the increasing menace of air attack, it became necessary to prepare for the blackout. Consequently the production areas at Willow Run were artificially lighted, thereby reversing Kahn's practice of providing maximum daylight.

Kahn also built the Curtis-Wright Corporation Plant in St. Louis and the Wright Aeronautical Plant in Cincinnati. When the use of structural steel was banned for such structures because of war shortages, he built plants with multiple-arch thin slab concrete roofs supported on concrete columns. Using this method of construction, he built the Pratt Whitney Missouri Plant in Kansas City and the Wright Aeronautical Corporation Plant No. 7 at Wood Ridge, New Jersey. Of

similar construction, the Dodge Chicago Plant (1943) for the manufacture of aircraft engines was the world's largest factory building. Even with such economies, the low, one-story units were handsome in their Spartan simplicity.

In addition to war plants, Kahn also built naval bases in Alaska, Hawaii, Midway, Puerto Rico, and at Jacksonville, Florida.

The strain of so much war work took its toll upon him. In 1942 he died of a bronchial ailment at the age of seventy-three. During his lifetime he was honored both in this country and abroad. In 1933 the University of Michigan conferred an honorary L.L.D. Degree upon him, and in 1942 he received an honorary Doctor of Fine Arts Degree from Syracuse University. In 1937 he received a gold medal at the International Exposition of Arts and Sciences in Paris and was made a chevalier of the Legion of Honor of France. The American Institute of Architects gave him a special award at its annual meeting in Detroit in 1942 and in the same year awarded him a medal for distinguished war service. The Franklin Institute awarded him posthumously the Frank P. Brown Medal in recognition of his outstanding achievements in the development of industrial architecture.

In a tribute to Kahn written after his death, architect Paul Cret wrote:

"It was my good fortune to enjoy Albert Kahn's friendship for twenty years and our conversations revealed his constant preoccupation with design. Each new work in his office was an occasion for experimenting with new materials, or with new ways to use old ones. In the current admiration for "big plants" and for mile-long facades, we must not forget that a selection from his minor work takes rank among the best of contemporary production, and marks the stages in his constant development.

"In a span of fifty years, as might be expected, there are changes in tendencies which reflect some of the influences to which he was subjected. The work of certain modern Germans, such as Ludwig Hoffman or Peter Behrens, have left their trace on some periods, while on others can be seen the orientation given to American architecture by McKim, Mead, and White.

"In his recent work, under the pressure of time, and with fitting recognition that war projects are not the place for experiments, he gave up architectural "embellishments" and retained only the play of contrasting masses, the patterns created by solids and voids, and his sensitive general lines. But among all the war construction, this is enough to mark the work of his office with the stamp of a master's hand.

"Albert Kahn was not a theorist: The 'architecture of tomorrow' had little interest for one so engrossed in creating the architecture of today. He had the humility of the good craftsman who puts forth his works as naturally and freely as an apple tree produces apples. He never courted honors or publicity, and when honors came, he accepted them with the most touching modesty.

"Generous in his appreciation of other men's work, and charitable in his readiness to help younger men, he was a force in the city which had become dearer to him than his birthplace.

"The profession, as a group, was slow in recognizing his worth; yet he was the best answer to our criticism in showing that the talent of the organizer, the clear vision of a businessman on current problems, are not incompatible with the creative mind of the artist and with his persistent quest for beauty."

Kahn either designed himself or closely supervised the design of every building he built. He once wrote: "Industrial architecture is 90 percent business and 10 percent art or science." If he was not a theorist like Louis Sullivan or Frank Lloyd Wright, his empirical method brought him closer to the fibre of modern society and led to solutions that were more far-reaching in their cumulative effect.

In a talk which Kahn gave in Detroit shortly before his death he said:

"Industrial architecture is continuing its forward march, contributing not only its share to the general welfare but winning recognition even in the field of art, which I dare say was perhaps the last it hoped for. But who would deny that large expanses of glass, for instance, essential in modern industrial building, have not exerted their influence on every day building—even in residential work? Or who would question that the entire field of architecture has been influenced by today's common sense solution of the factory building?"

MORET
9.18.24.

Sketch of Moret, France, by Albert Kahn, 1924

I. Pre-Industrial Architecture
1888-1908

Note: Photo credit AKA denotes Albert Kahn Associates, Inc., Architects & Engineers

Fig. 1 *Gilbert Lee House—*
View of Entrance
Mason & Rice
Detroit, Michigan, 1888
PHOTO: ELMER L. ASTLEFORD

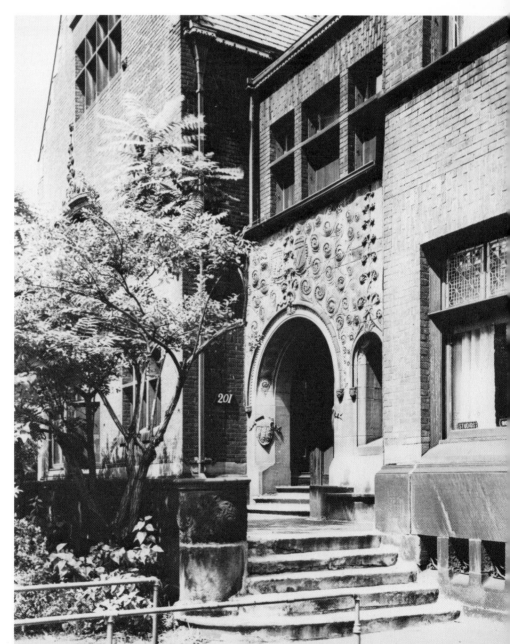

Fig. 2 *Dexter M. Ferry Farm—Residence*
Mason & Rice
Unadilla, New York, 1890
PHOTO: COURTESY MRS. C. C. DAVIS

Fig. 3 *Dexter M. Ferry Farm—*
Farmer's Lodge
Mason & Rice
Unadilla, New York, 1890
PHOTO: COURTESY MRS. C. C. DAVIS

Fig. 4   *Dexter M. Ferry Farm—Horse Barn*
Mason & Rice
Unadilla, New York, 1890
PHOTO: COURTESY MRS. C. C. DAVIS

Fig. 5   *William Livingstone House*
Mason & Rice
Detroit, Michigan, 1893
PHOTO: ELMER L. ASTLEFORD

Fig. 6   *Watson M. Freer House*
Mason & Rice
Detroit, Michigan, 1895
PHOTO: GEORGE D. MASON

Fig. 7   *Hiram Walker*
& Sons
Mason & Rice
Windsor, Ontario, 1894
PHOTO: HENRY A. LEUNG

Fig. 8 *Children's Hospital*
Nettleton, Kahn & Trowbridge
Detroit, Michigan, 1896

PHOTO: AKA

Fig. 9 *Scripps Library and Art Gallery*
Nettleton & Kahn
Detroit, Michigan, 1898

PHOTO: THE DETROIT INSTITUTE OF ARTS

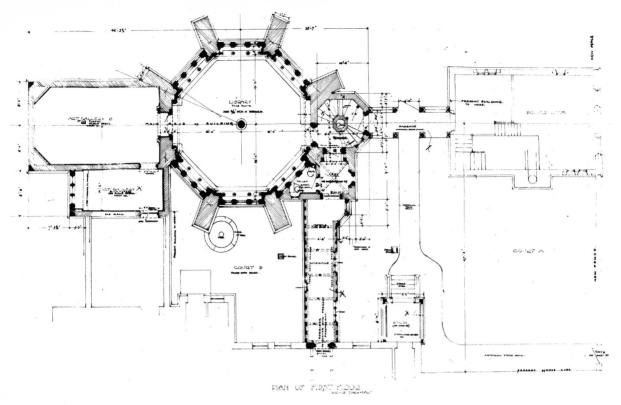

Fig. 10 *Scripps Library and Art Gallery—Plan*
Nettleton & Kahn
Detroit, Michigan, 1898
PHOTO: THE DETROIT INSTITUTE OF ARTS

Fig. 11 *Scripps Library and Art Gallery—Cross Section*
Nettleton & Kahn
Detroit, Michigan, 1898
PHOTO: THE DETROIT INSTITUTE OF ARTS

Fig. 12   *Scripps Library and Art Gallery—Interior of Library*
Nettleton & Kahn
Detroit, Michigan, 1898
PHOTO: THE DETROIT INSTITUTE OF ARTS

Fig. 13   *Palms Apartment House*
Mason & Kahn
Detroit, Michigan, 1902
PHOTO: HENRY A. LEUNG

Fig. 14   *Temple Beth El*
Mason & Kahn
Detroit, Michigan, 1903
PHOTO: AKA

Fig. 15   *Temple Beth El—Interior*
Mason & Kahn
Detroit, Michigan, 1903
PHOTO: AKA

Fig. 16   *Temple Beth El—Plaster Details*
Mason & Kahn
Detroit, Michigan, 1903
PHOTO: AKA

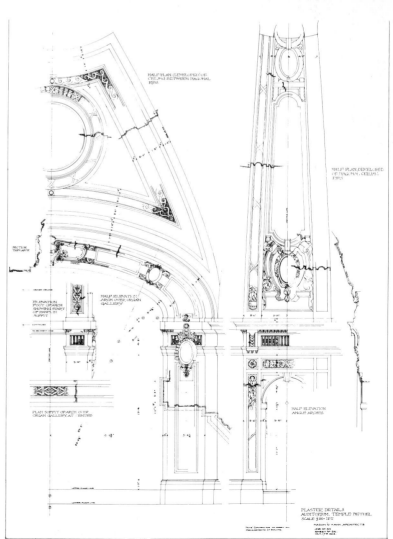

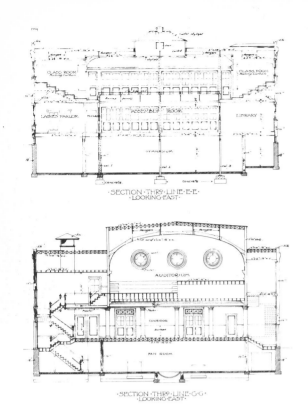

SECTION·THRO·LINE·E·E·
LOOKING·EAST·

SECTION·THRO·LINE·G·G·
LOOKING·EAST·

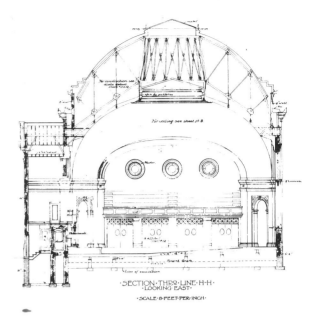

SECTION·THRO·LINE·H·H·
LOOKING·EAST·

·SCALE·8·FEET·PER·INCH·

Fig. 17   *Temple Beth El—Sections*
Mason & Kahn
Detroit, Michigan, 1903
PHOTO: AKA

Fig. 18   *Conservatory*
Belle Isle Park
Detroit, Michigan, 1903
PHOTO: JOSEPH P. MESSANA

Fig. 19   *Casino*
Belle Isle Park
Detroit, Michigan, 1908
PHOTO: JOSEPH P. MESSANA

Fig. 20   *Engineering Building*
University of Michigan
Ann Arbor, Michigan, 1903
PHOTO: HENRY A. LEUNG

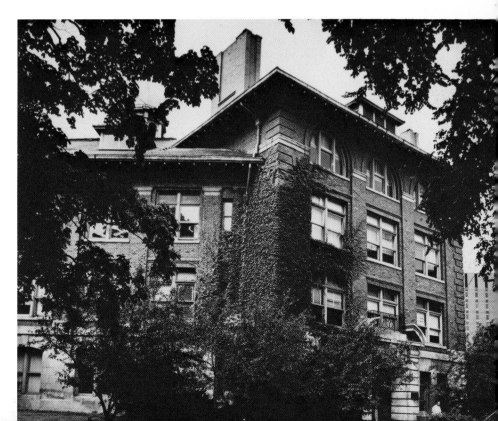

II. Early Industrial Architecture 1901-1921

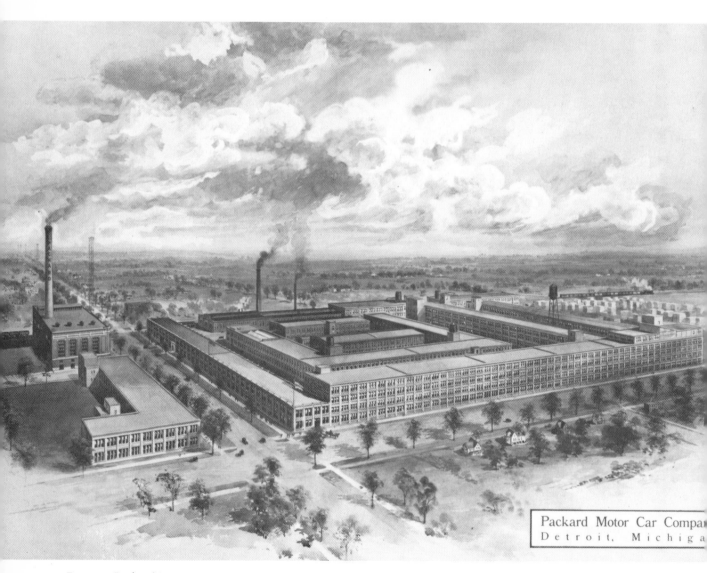

Fig. 21 *Packard Motor Car Company*
Detroit, Michigan, 1903
PHOTO: AKA

Fig. 22   *Packard Motor Car Company Building No. 10*
Detroit, Michigan, 1905

PHOTO: J. McCAUGHEY

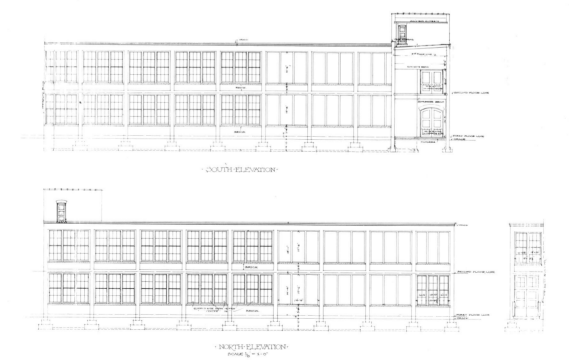

· SOUTH · ELEVATION ·

· NORTH · ELEVATION ·
SCALE ⅛" = 1'-0"

Fig. 23   *Packard Motor Car Company Building No. 10—Elevations*
Detroit, Michigan, 1905

PHOTO: COPYCRAFT

Fig. 24   *Packard Motor Car Company Building No. 10—Interior*
Detroit, Michigan, 1905
PHOTO: AKA

Fig. 25   *Grabowsky Power
Wagon Company*
Detroit, Michigan, 1907
PHOTO: MANNING BROS.

Fig. 26   *Chalmers Motor Car Company*
Detroit, Michigan, 1907
PHOTO: CHRYSLER CORPORATION

Fig. 27   *Mergenthaler*
Linotype Company
Brooklyn, New York, 1907
PHOTO: AKA

Fig. 28 *Ford Motor Company*
Highland Park Plant
Highland Park, Michigan
PHOTO: AKA

Fig. 29 *Ford Motor Company—Original Building*
Highland Park Plant
Highland Park, Michigan, 1909
PHOTO: AKA

Fig. 30   *Ford Motor Company—Interior of Original Building*
Highland Park Plant
Highland Park, Michigan, 1909
PHOTO: AKA

Fig. 31   *Ford Motor Company—*
Ventilating Skylights
Over Machine Shop
Highland Park Plant
Highland Park, Michigan, 1909
PHOTO: AKA

Fig. 32 *Ford Motor Company—Automobile Storage Area*
Highland Park Plant
Highland Park, Michigan, 1909
PHOTO: AKA

Fig. 33 *Ford Motor Company—*
Office Building
Highland Park Plant
Highland Park, Michigan, 1910
PHOTO: AKA

Fig. 34   *Ford Motor Company—Mock-up of Body Assembly Line*
Highland Park Plant
Highland Park, Michigan, 1914-15

PHOTO: AKA

Fig. 35   *Ford Motor Company—Interior*
Highland Park Plant
Highland Park, Michigan, 1913

PHOTO: AKA

Fig. 36 *Ford Motor Company*
Highland Park Plant
Highland Park, Michigan, 1918
PHOTO: AKA

Fig. 37 *Ford Motor Company—Interior*
Highland Park Plant
Highland Park, Michigan, 1918
PHOTO: AKA

Fig. 38   *Hudson Motor Car Company—Office Building*
Detroit, Michigan, 1910
PHOTO: MANNING BROTHERS

Fig. 39   *Continental Motors Corporation*   Fig. 40   *Interior* (below)
Detroit, Michigan, 1912
PHOTO: MANNING BROTHERS

Fig. 41   *Dodge Brothers Corporation*
Hamtramck, Michigan
PHOTO: CHRYSLER CORPORATION

Fig. 42   *Dodge Brothers Corporation—View Between Buildings*
Hamtramck, Michigan, 1910
PHOTO: AKA

Fig. 43   *Dodge Brothers Corporation—Interior*
Hamtramck, Michigan, 1910
PHOTO: AKA

Fig. 44   *Burroughs Adding Machine Company*
Detroit, Michigan, 1912-19
PHOTO: MANNING BROTHERS

Fig. 45   *Fisher Body Company*
Cleveland, Ohio, 1921
PHOTO: AKA

Fig. 46   *Buick Motor Car Company—Interior*
Flint, Michigan, 1919
PHOTO: AKA

Fig. 47   *Packard Motor Car Company—Interior of Forge Building*
Detroit, Michigan, 1910
PHOTO: MANNING BROTHERS

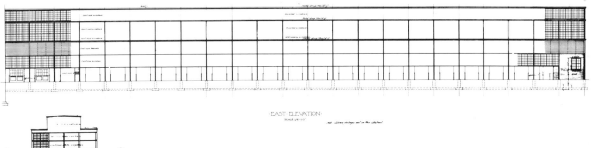

Fig. 48   *Packard Motor Car Company—Side and End Elevations*
Detroit, Michigan, 1910
PHOTO: AKA

III. Early Commercial Architecture 1907-1917

Fig. 49   *The Trussed Concrete Building* (The Owen Building) Detroit, Michigan, 1907

PHOTO: AKA

Fig. 50   *Grinnell Brothers Building*
Detroit, Michigan, 1908
PHOTO: MANNING BROTHERS

Fig. 51   *National Theatre*
Detroit, Michigan, 1910
PHOTO: AKA

Fig. 52 *National Theatre—Night View*
Detroit, Michigan, 1910
PHOTO: AKA

Fig. 53 *Palmer Office and Store Building*
Detroit, Michigan, 1910
PHOTO: MANNING BROTHERS

Fig. 54 *Ford Motor Company Service Building*
(Boulevard Building)
Detroit, Michigan, 1913
PHOTO: MANNING BROTHERS

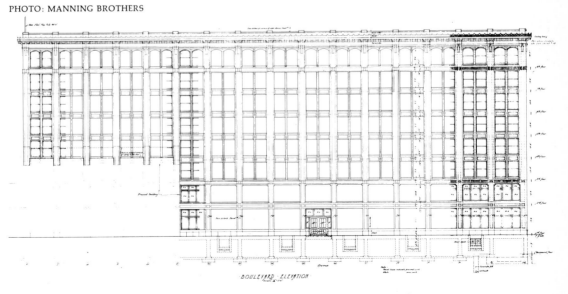

BOULEVARD ELEVATION

Fig. 55 *Ford Motor Company Service Building—Boulevard Elevation*
(Boulevard Building)
Detroit, Michigan, 1913
PHOTO: AKA

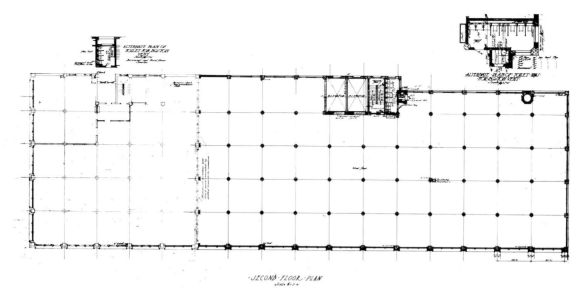

·SECOND·FLOOR·PLAN·

Fig. 56 *Ford Motor Company Service Building—Plan*
(Boulevard Building)
Detroit, Michigan, 1913
PHOTO: AKA

Fig. 57 *Detroit Free Press Building*
(Now Transportation Building)
Detroit, Michigan, 1913
PHOTO: JOSEPH P. MESSANA

Fig. 58   *Kresge Building*
Detroit, Michigan, 1914
PHOTO: MANNING BROTHERS

Fig. 59   *Vinton Building*
Detroit, Michigan, 1917
PHOTO: JOSEPH P. MESSANA

Fig. 60   *A. Krolik & Company*
Warehouse
Detroit, Michigan, 1916
PHOTO: MANNING BROTHERS

Fig. 61   *Detroit News*
Detroit, Michigan, 1915
PHOTO: MANNING BROTHERS

Fig. 62   *Hudson Motor Car Company—Display Room Interior*
Detroit, Michigan, 1910
PHOTO: THOMAS ELLISON

IV. Early Institutional Architecture 1913-1919

Fig. 63   *Hill Auditorium*
University of Michigan
Ann Arbor, Michigan, 1913
PHOTO: HEDRICH-BLESSING

Fig. 64   *Hill Auditorium—*
Side Entrance
University of Michigan
Ann Arbor, Michigan, 1913
PHOTO: HENRY A. LEUNG

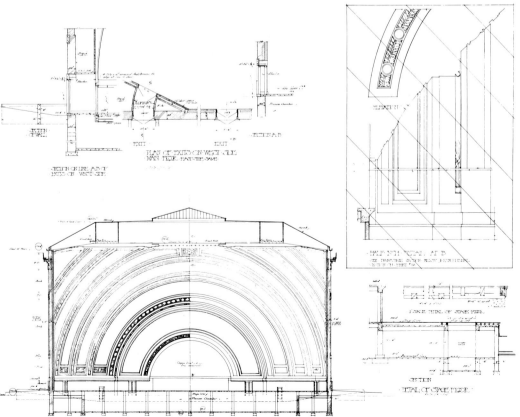

Fig. 65   *Hill Auditorium—*
Transverse Section
University of Michigan
Ann Arbor, Michigan, 1913
PHOTO: AKA

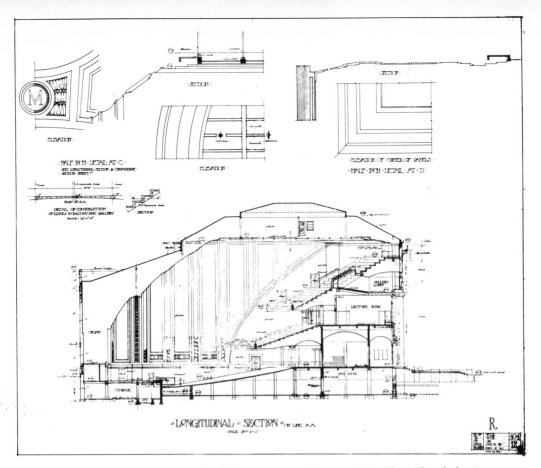

Fig. 66   *Hill Auditorium—Longitudinal Section*   Fig. 67   *Main Floor Plan* (below)
University of Michigan, Ann Arbor, Michigan, 1913, PHOTO: AKA

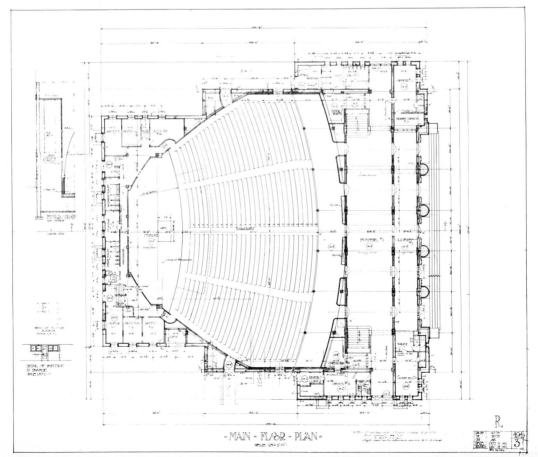

Fig. 68 *Natural Science Building*
University of Michigan
Ann Arbor, Michigan, 1917

PHOTO: HENRY A. LEUNG

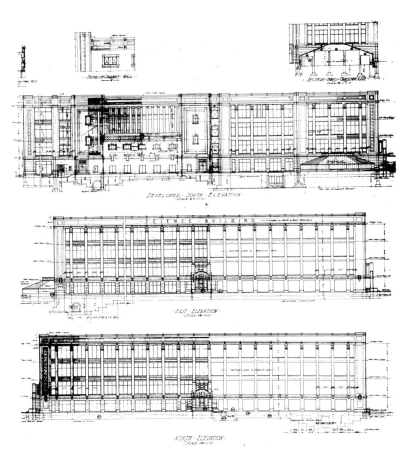

Fig. 69 *Natural Science Building—Elevations*
University of Michigan
Ann Arbor, Michigan, 1917

PHOTO: AKA

Fig. 70   *Natural Science Building—*
Brick Detail
University of Michigan
Ann Arbor, Michigan, 1917
PHOTO: HENRY A. LEUNG

Fig. 71   *Natural Science Building—*
Second Floor Plan
University of Michigan
Ann Arbor, Michigan, 1917
PHOTO: AKA

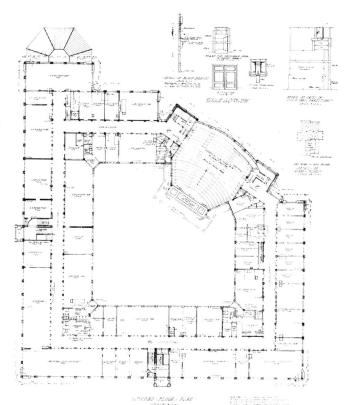

Fig. 72 *General Library*
University of Michigan
Ann Arbor, Michigan, 1919
PHOTO: HENRY A. LEUNG

Fig. 73 *U.S. Aviation School—Laboratory Building*
Langley Field, Virginia, 1917
PHOTO: STUART HAWKINS

Fig. 74   *U. S. Aviation School—Laboratory Building, Detail of Entrance*
Langley Field, Virginia, 1917

Fig. 75   *U.S. Aviation School—Laboratory Building, Detail of West Facade*
Langley Field, Virginia, 1917

Fig. 76 *Hangar*
Langley Field, Virginia, 1917
PHOTO: AKA

Fig. 77 *Grosse Pointe Shores Village Hall*
Grosse Pointe Shores, Michigan, 1915
PHOTO: JOSEPH P. MESSANA

V. Early Residential Architecture
1903-1917

Fig. 78   *Charles M. Swift House—Entrance Front*
Fig. 79   *Side Facing Lake* (below)
Grosse Pointe, Michigan, 1903
PHOTO: MANNING BROTHERS

Fig. 80   *E. Chandler Walker House—Entrance Front*
Windsor, Ontario, 1905
PHOTO: JOHN S. COBURN

Fig. 81   *E. Chandler Walker House—Side Facing Garden*
Windsor, Ontario, 1905
PHOTO: ALLEN STROSS

Fig. 82   E. Chandler Walker House—East Front Elevation
Fig. 83   First Floor Plan (below)
Windsor, Ontario, 1905
PHOTO: AKA

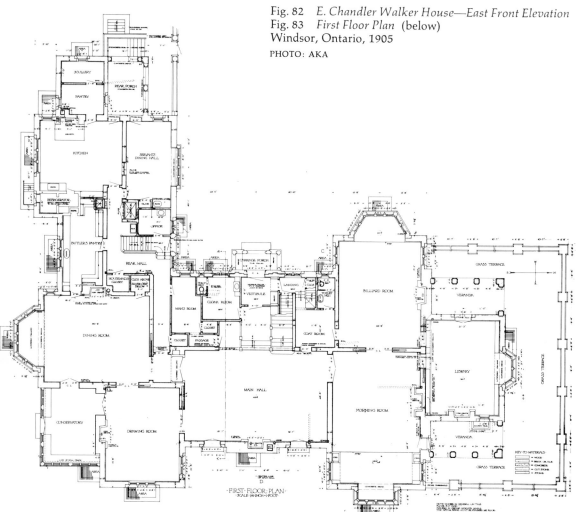

Fig. 84   *Albert Kahn House—Entrance Front*
Detroit, Michigan, 1907
PHOTO: AKA

Fig. 85   *Albert Kahn House—Entrance*
Detroit, Michigan, 1907
PHOTO: AKA

Fig. 86   *Albert Kahn House—*
Interior, Hall Showing Stairs
Detroit, Michigan, 1907
PHOTO: AKA

Fig. 87   *Albert Kahn Hous*
Interior, Hall Looking Towa
Living Room
Detroit, Michigan, 1907
PHOTO: AKA

Fig. 88 *Albert Kahn House—Interior, Dining Room*
Detroit, Michigan, 1907
PHOTO: AKA

Fig. 89 *George G. Booth House—Entrance Front*
Cranbrook House, Bloomfield Hills, Michigan, 1907
PHOTO: HENRY A. LEUNG

Fig. 90 *George G. Booth House*
Cranbrook House
Bloomfield Hills, Michigan, 1907
PHOTO: HARVEY CROZE

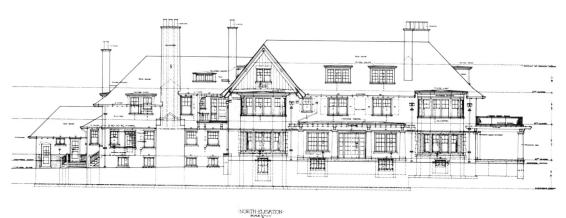

·NORTH·ELEVATION·

Fig. 91 *George G. Booth House—North Elevation*
Fig. 92 *First Floor Plan*
Cranbrook House, Bloomfield Hills, Michigan, 1907
PHOTO: AKA

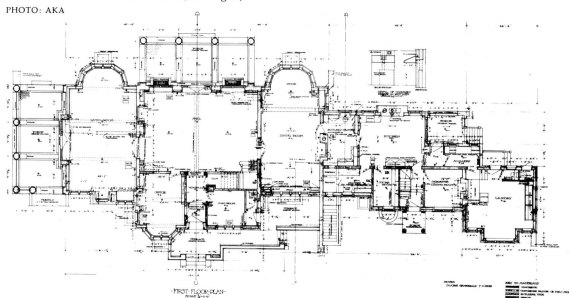

·FIRST·FLOOR·PLAN·

Fig. 93   *William L. Clements House*
Bay City, Michigan, 1908
PHOTO: AKA

Fig. 94   *William L. Clements House—Interior*
Bay City, Michigan, 1908
PHOTO: AKA

Fig. 95   *Horace Elgin Dodge House—
Entrance Front*
Grosse Pointe, Michigan, 1910
PHOTO: AKA

Fig. 96   *Horace Elgin Dodge*
House—Side Facing Lake
Fig. 97   *Interior, Hall*
Showing Stairs
Grosse Pointe, Michigan, 1910
PHOTO: AKA

Fig. 98 *Horace Elgin*
Dodge House—Interior,
Hall Showing
Fireplace
Grosse Pointe, Michigan, 1910
PHOTO: AKA

Fig. 99 *Horace Elgin*
Dodge House—Interior,
Dining Room
Grosse Pointe, Michigan, 1910
PHOTO: AKA

Fig. 100   *Detroit Golf Club—Entrance Front*
Detroit, Michigan, 1916
PHOTO: HEDRICH-BLESSING

Fig. 101   *Detroit Golf Club—Side Facing Golf Course*
Detroit, Michigan, 1916
PHOTO: MANNING BROTHERS

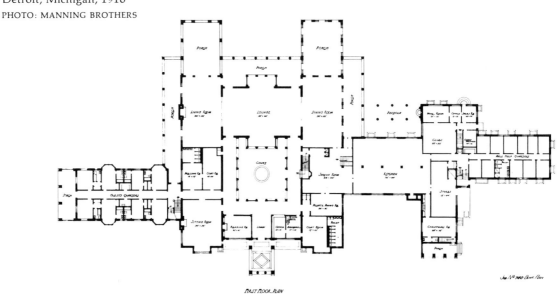

Fig. 102   *Detroit Golf Club—First Floor Plan*
Detroit, Michigan, 1916
PHOTO: AKA

Fig. 103   *Country Club of Detroit—Entrance Front*
Grosse Pointe Farms, Michigan, 1905

Fig. 104   *Country Club of Detroit—Side Facing Lake*
Grosse Pointe Farms, Michigan, 1905

Fig. 105   *Henry B. Joy House—Side Facing Lake*
Fig. 106   *First Floor Plan* (below)
Grosse Pointe Farms, Michigan, 1908
PHOTO: MANNING BROTHERS·

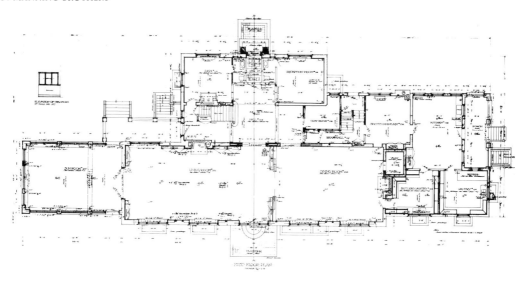

Fig. 107   *Philip McMillan House—Lake Side of House*
Grosse Pointe Farms, Michigan, 1912
PHOTO: ALLEN STROSS

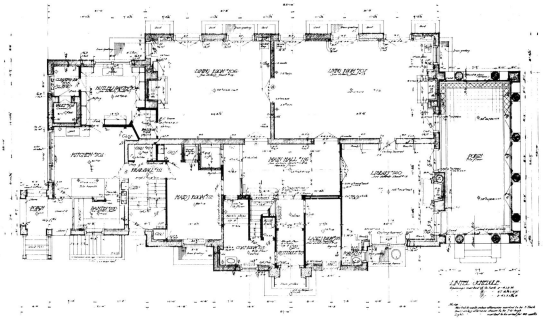

Fig. 108 *Philip McMillan House—First Floor Plan*
Grosse Pointe Farms, Michigan, 1912
PHOTO: AKA

Fig. 109 *C. Goodloe Edgar House—Lake Side of House*
Grosse Pointe Shores, Michigan, 1915
PHOTO: HENRY A. LEUNG

Fig. 110 *John S. Newberry House—Entrance Front*
Grosse Pointe Farms, Michigan, 1915
PHOTO: MANNING BROTHERS

·SOUTH·ELEVATION·

Fig. 111 *John S. Newberry House—South Elevation*
Grosse Pointe Farms, Michigan, 1915
PHOTO: AKA

Fig. 112   *John S. Newberry
House—Entrance*
Grosse Pointe Farms, Michigan, 1915
PHOTO: AKA

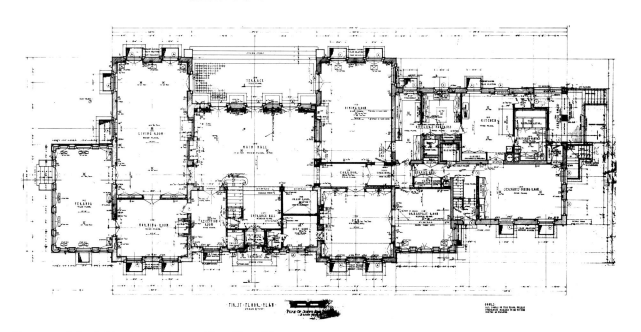

Fig. 113   *John S. Newberry House—First Floor Plan*
Grosse Pointe Farms, Michigan, 1915
PHOTO: AKA

Fig. 114   *John S. Newberry House—*
Interior, Main Hall
Grosse Pointe Farms, Michigan, 1915
PHOTO: AKA

Fig. 115   *John S. Newberry House—*
Interior, Staircase
Grosse Pointe Farms, Michigan, 1915
PHOTO: AKA

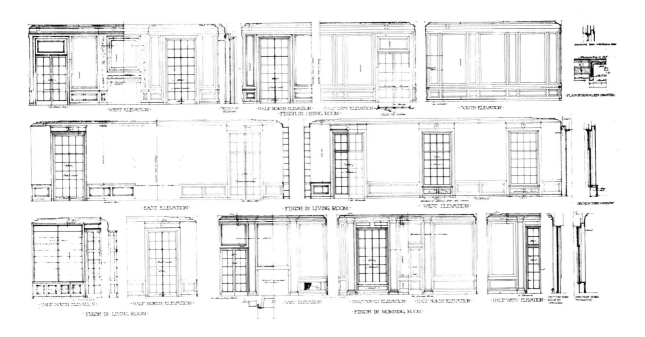

Fig. 116   *John S. Newberry House—Dining Room and Living Room Finish*
Grosse Pointe Farms, Michigan, 1915

PHOTO: AKA

Fig. 117   *John S. Newberry House—Interior, Living Room Showing Fireplace*
Grosse Pointe Farms, Michigan, 1915

PHOTO: AKA

Fig. 118   *John S. Newberry House—Interior, Living Room Showing Bookcase*
Grosse Pointe Farms, Michigan, 1915
PHOTO: AKA

Fig. 119   *John S. Newberry House—Interior, Veranda*
Grosse Pointe Farms, Michigan, 1915
PHOTO: AKA

Fig. 120   *John S. Newberry House—North Elevation*
Grosse Pointe Farms, Michigan, 1915
PHOTO: AKA

Fig. 121   *Frank and Robert Kuhn House*
Grosse Pointe Farms, Michigan, 1914
PHOTO: HENRY A. LEUNG

Fig. 122 *Frank L. Klingensmith House—Entrance Front*
Bloomfield Hills, Michigan, 1916
PHOTO: MANNING BROTHERS

Fig. 123 Frank L. Klingensmith House—Side Facing Garden
Bloomfield Hills, Michigan, 1916
PHOTO: MANNING BROTHERS

Fig. 124 *Albert Kahn Summer Cottage— Side Facing Garden* Walnut Lake, Oakland County, Michigan, 1917

PHOTO: AKA

Fig. 125 *Albert Kahn Summer Cottage — Entrance* Walnut Lake, Oakland County, Michigan, 1917

PHOTO: AKA

Fig. 126 *Albert Kahn Summer Cottage — View of Garden and Lake* Walnut Lake, Oakland County, Michigan, 1917

PHOTO: AKA

VI. Late Institutional and Public Architecture 1915-1927

Fig. 127 *Detroit Athletic Club*
Detroit, Michigan, 1915
PHOTO: HEDRICH-BLESSING

Fig. 128 *Detroit Athletic Club—Interior*
Detroit, Michigan, 1915

Fig. 129 *Police Headquarters*
Detroit, Michigan, 1921

Fig. 130   *University Hospital*
University of Michigan
Ann Arbor, Michigan, 1920
PHOTO: HEDRICH-BLESSING

Fig. 131   *University Hospital—*
Plot Plan
University of Michigan
Ann Arbor, Michigan, 1920
PHOTO: AKA

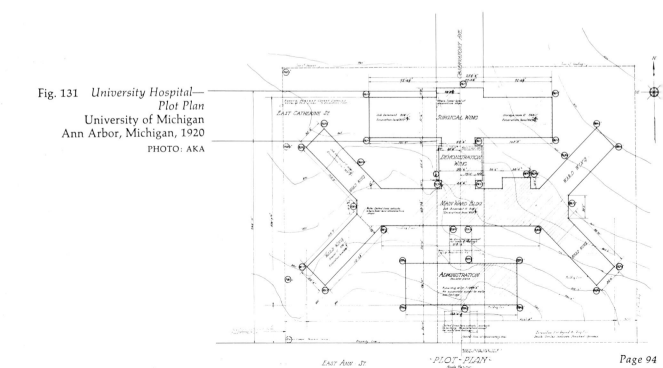

Fig. 132 *Medical Building*
University of Michigan
Ann Arbor, Michigan, 1925
PHOTO: AKA

Fig. 133 *Angell Hall*
University of Michigan
Ann Arbor, Michigan, 1922
PHOTO: THOMAS ELLISON

Fig. 134 *William L. Clements Library*
University of Michigan
Ann Arbor, Michigan, 1922
PHOTO: HEDRICH-BLESSING

Fig. 135 *Temple Beth El*
Detroit, Michigan, 1927
PHOTO: HEDRICH-BLESSING

VII. Late Commercial Architecture 1915-1939

Fig. 136   *Detroit Trust Company*
Detroit, Michigan, 1915
PHOTO: HEDRICH-BLESSING

Fig. 137   *Detroit Trust Company — Interior*
Detroit, Michigan, 1915
PHOTO: THOMAS ELLISON

Fig. 138   *Packard Sales Room*
Detroit, Michigan, 1915
PHOTO: AKA

Fig. 139 *Ford Motor Company —*
Interior
Main Sales Room
New York, New York, 1917
PHOTO: AKA

Fig. 140 *National Bank of Detroit*
Detroit, Michigan, 1922
PHOTO: HEDRICH-BLESSING

Fig. 141
*National Bank
of Detroit—
Drawing of
Interior by
Ivan Dise*
Detroit, Michigan, 1922
PHOTO: MANNING BROTHERS

Fig. 142 *General Motors
Building*
Detroit, Michigan, 1922
PHOTO: AKA

Fig. 143 *General Motors Building — Main Entrance*
Detroit, Michigan, 1922
PHOTO: JOHN WALLACE GILLIES

Fig. 144 *General Motors Building — Foyer*
Detroit, Michigan, 1922
PHOTO: G. M. PHOTOGRAPHIC

Fig. 145 *Detroit Free Press*
Detroit, Michigan, 1925
PHOTO: HEDRICH-BLESSING

Fig. 146 *Maccabees Building*
Detroit, Michigan, 1927
PHOTO: THOMAS ELLISON

Fig. 147 *Fisher Building*
Detroit, Michigan, 1927
PHOTO: HEDRICH-BLESSING

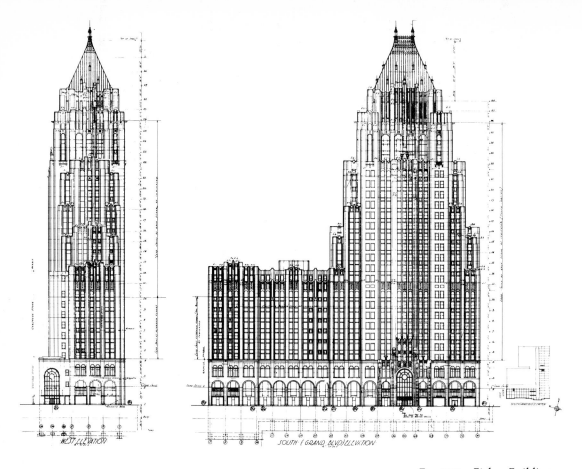

Fig. 148　Fisher Building —
West and South Elevations
Detroit, Michigan, 1927

PHOTO: AKA

Fig. 149　Fisher Building —
Interior, General View of
Main Corridor
Detroit, Michigan, 1927

PHOTO: OWNER

Fig. 150   *Ford Motor Company*
Rotunda Building
Dearborn, Michigan, 1933
PHOTO: FORD PHOTOGRAPHIC

Fig. 151   *Ford Exposition Building*
New York World's Fair, 1939
PHOTO: AKA

VIII. Late Residential Architecture
1926-1928

Fig. 152   *Edsel B. Ford House — Entrance Front*
Grosse Pointe Shores, Michigan, 1926
PHOTO: DETROIT NEWS

Fig. 153   *Edsel B. Ford House — Side Facing Lake*
Grosse Pointe Shores, Michigan, 1926
PHOTO: THOMAS ELLISON

Fig. 154   *Edsel B. Ford House — Courtyard at Side of House*
Grosse Pointe Shores, Michigan, 1926
PHOTO: AKA

Fig. 155 *Alvan Macauley House — Side Facing Lake*
Grosse Pointe Shores, Michigan, 1928
PHOTO: MANNING BROTHERS

Fig. 156 *Alvan Macauley
House — Entrance Front*
Grosse Pointe Shores, Michigan, 1928
PHOTO: THOMAS ELLISON

Fig. 157 *Alvan Macauley
House — First Floor Plan*
Grosse Pointe Shores, Michigan, 1928
PHOTO: AKA

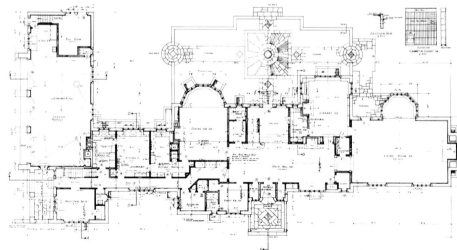

Fig. 158 *Alvan Macauley House — Interior, Hall and Staircase*
Grosse Pointe Shores, Michigan, 1928
PHOTO: THOMAS ELLISON

Fig. 159 *Alvan Macauley House — Interior, Living Room*
Grosse Pointe Shores, Michigan, 1928
PHOTO: THOMAS ELLISON

Fig. 160 *James Couzens House — Entrance Front*
Bloomfield Hills, Michigan, 1928
PHOTO: COURTESY MRS. WILLIAM YAW

Fig. 161 *Albert Kahn House Addition — Interior*
General View Showing Fireplace
and Bay Window
Detroit, Michigan, 1928
PHOTO: THOMAS ELLISON

Fig. 162   *Albert Kahn House Addition — Interior, Fireplace*
Detroit, Michigan, 1928
PHOTO: THOMAS ELLISON

Fig. 163   *Albert Kahn House Addition — Interior, Showing Tapestry*
Detroit, Michigan, 1928
PHOTO: THOMAS ELLISON

Fig. 164   *Albert Kahn House Addition — Interior, Showing Piano*
Detroit, Michigan, 1928
PHOTO: AKA

Fig. 165   *At the Breaking of Ground for The Detroit Institute of Arts*
Detroit, Michigan, June 22, 1922
PHOTO: DETROIT INSTITUTE OF ARTS

IX. Late Industrial Architecture
1917-1943

Fig. 166 *Ford Motor Company — Building B*
Rouge Plant, Dearborn, Michigan, 1917
PHOTO: FORD MUSEUM

Fig. 167 *Ford Motor Company*
Rouge Plant, Dearborn, Michigan
PHOTO: FORD MUSEUM

Fig. 168 *Ford Motor Company — Main Power House*
Rouge Plant
Dearborn, Michigan, 1921
PHOTO: AKA

Fig. 169 *Ford Motor Company — Glass Plant*
Rouge Plant, Dearborn, Michigan, 1924
PHOTO: AKA

Fig. 170 *Ford Motor Company — Open Hearth Mills*
Rouge Plant
Dearborn, Michigan, 1924-25
PHOTO: AKA

Fig. 171 *Ford Motor Company — Engineering Laboratory*
Dearborn, Michigan, 1925
PHOTO: MR. EBLING

Fig. 172 *Ford Motor Company — Interior, Engineering Laboratory*
Dearborn, Michigan, 1925
PHOTO: FORD MOTOR COMPANY

Fig. 173 *Ford Motor Company —
Engineering Laboratory Power House*
Dearborn, Michigan, 1925
PHOTO: FORD MOTOR COMPANY

Fig. 174   *Hudson Motor Company — Office Building*
Detroit, Michigan, 1931
PHOTO: THOMAS ELLISON

Fig. 175
Chrysler Corporation
Plymouth Plant
Detroit, Michigan, 1928
PHOTO: CHRYSLER CORPORATION

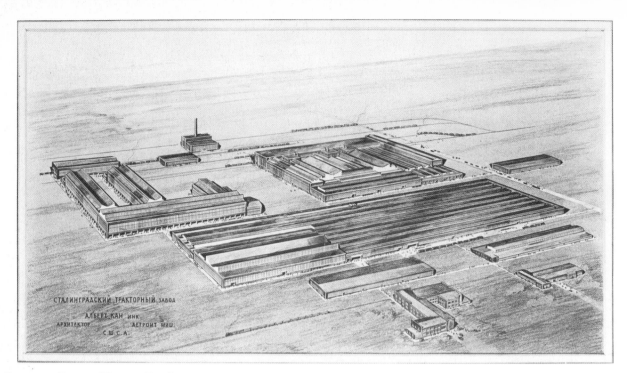

Fig. 176   *Tractor Plant — Rendering*
Stalingrad, Russia, 1930
PHOTO: JEFFERY WHITE STUDIOS

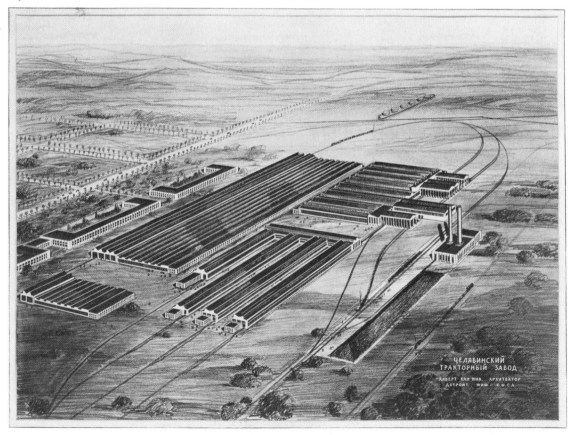

Fig. 177   *Tractor Plant — Rendering*
Cheliabinsk, Russia, 1933
PHOTO: JEFFERY WHITE STUDIOS

Fig. 178   *Tractor Plant — Interior*
Cheliabinsk, Russia, 1933
PHOTO: AKA

Fig. 179   *Republic Steel Corporation —*
Interior, Hot and
Cold Strip Mills
Cleveland, Ohio, 1936
PHOTO: DAMORA

Fig. 180 *Republic Steel Corporation — Interior, Hot and Cold Strip Mills*
Cleveland, Ohio, 1936

PHOTO: DAMORA

Fig. 181 *Ford Motor Company — Tire Plant*
Rouge Plant
Dearborn, Michigan, 1936

PHOTO: FORD MOTOR COMPANY

Fig. 182   *Ford Motor Company —*
Interior, Tire Plant
Rouge Plant
Dearborn, Michigan, 1936
PHOTO: FORD MOTOR COMPANY

Fig. 183   *Kelvinator Corporation — Warehouse*
Plymouth, Michigan, 1936
PHOTO: HEDRICH-BLESSING

Fig. 184   *General Motors Corporation — Manufacturing Plant*
Diesel Engine Division
Detroit, Michigan, 1937
PHOTO: HEDRICH-BLESSING

Fig. 185   *Lady Esther Plant*
Clearing, Illinois, 1938
PHOTO: HEDRICH-BLESSING

Fig. 186   *Chrysler Corporation — Press Shop*
DeSoto Division
Detroit, Michigan, 1936

PHOTO: HEDRICH-BLESSING

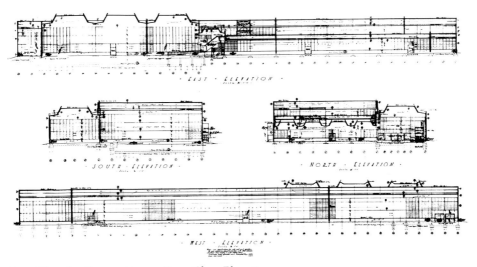

Fig. 187   *Chrysler Corporation — Press Shop Elevations*
Fig. 188   *Press Shop Sections* (below)
DeSoto Division, Detroit, Michigan, 1936

PHOTO: AKA

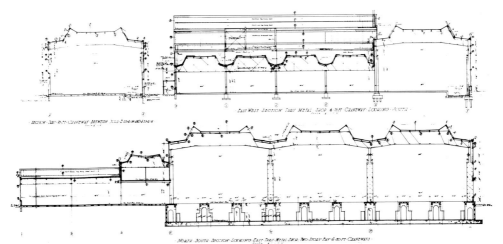

Fig. 189   *Chrysler Corporation — Half-Ton Truck Plant Assembly Building*
Dodge Division
Warren, Michigan, 1938
PHOTO: HEDRICH-BLESSING

Fig. 190   *Chrysler Corporation —*
Half-Ton Truck Plant
Interior
Dodge Division
Warren, Michigan, 1938
PHOTO: HEDRICH-BLESSING

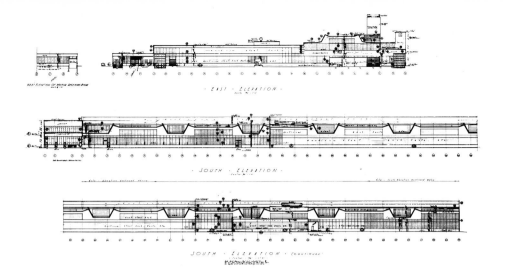

Fig. 191   *Chrysler Corporation — Half-Ton Truck Plant Elevations*
Fig. 192   *Sections* (below)
Dodge Division, Warren, Michigan, 1938

PHOTO: AKA

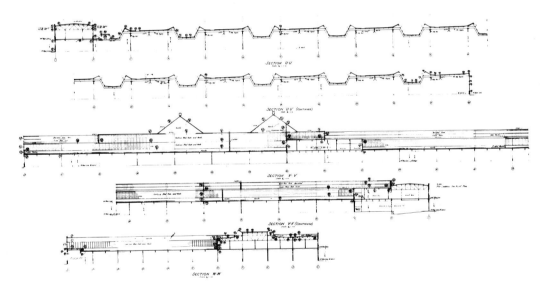

Fig. 193   *Chrysler Corporation — Half-Ton Truck Plant, Export Building*
Dodge Division, Warren, Michigan, 1938

PHOTO: HEDRICH-BLESSING

Fig. 194   *Ohio Steel Foundry Company — Roll and Heavy Machine Shop*
Fig. 195   *Interior* (right)
Lima, Ohio, 1938
PHOTO: HEDRICH-BLESSING

Fig. 196   *Glenn L. Martin Company — Addition to Manufacturing Building*
Baltimore, Maryland, 1937
PHOTO: OWNER

Fig. 197   *Glenn L. Martin Company —*
Addition to
Assembly Building
Baltimore, Maryland, 1937
PHOTO: DAMORA

Fig. 198   *Glenn L. Martin Company —*
Interior
Baltimore, Maryland, 1937
PHOTO: OWNER

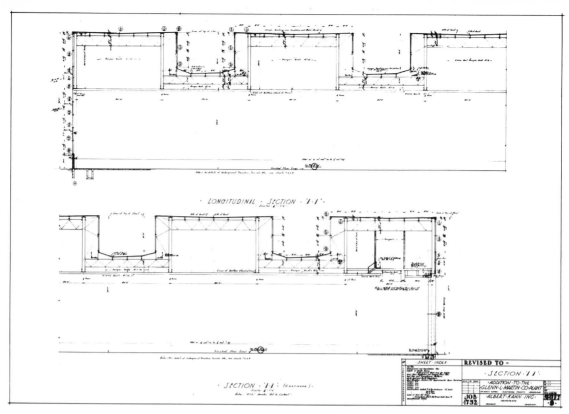

Fig. 199 *Glenn L. Martin Company — Section AA*   **Fig. 200** *Section BB* (below)
Baltimore, Maryland, 1937

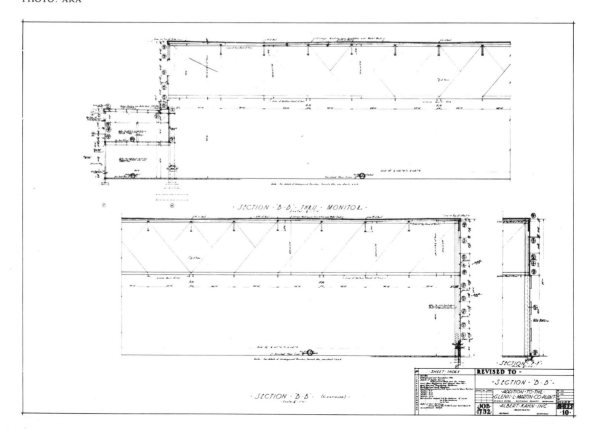

Fig. 201 *Burroughs Adding Machine Company — Office and Factory*
Plymouth, Michigan, 1938
PHOTO: HEDRICH-BLESSING

Fig. 202 *Ford Motor Company — Press Shop*
Rouge Plant
Dearborn, Michigan, 1939
PHOTO: FORD MOTOR COMPANY

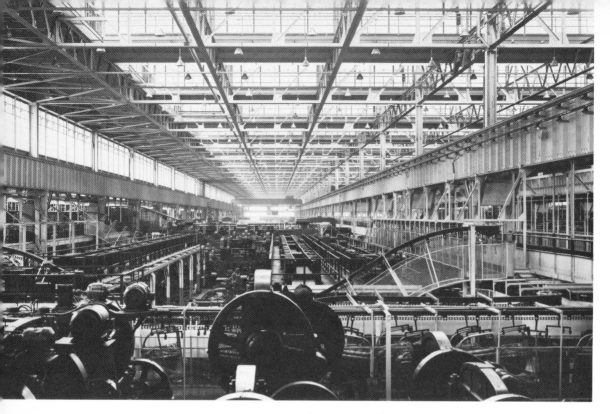

Fig. 203　*Ford Motor Company — Interior, Press Shop*
Rouge Plant, Dearborn, Michigan, 1939
PHOTO: FORD MOTOR COMPANY

Fig. 204　*Chrysler Corporation*
Tank Arsenal
Warren, Michigan, 1941
PHOTO: HEDRICH-BLESSING

Fig. 205   *Chrysler Corporation — Interior*
Tank Arsenal
Warren, Michigan, 1941
PHOTO: HEDRICH-BLESSING

Fig. 206   *American Steel Foundries — Cast Armor Plant — Foundry from Northeast*
East Chicago, Indiana, 1941
PHOTO: HEDRICH-BLESSING

Fig. 207 *American Locomotive Company — Factory (Machine Shop)* Auburn, New York, 1942
PHOTO: HEDRICH-BLESSING

Fig. 208 *American Locomotive Company — Factory (Machine Shop) Interior* Auburn, New York, 1942
PHOTO: HEDRICH-BLESSING

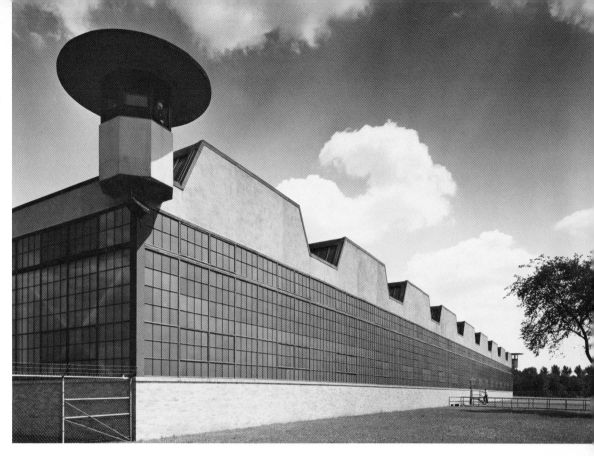

Fig. 209   *The Amertorp Corporation — Ordnance Plant — Torpedo Plant*
Chicago, Illinois, 1942
PHOTO: HEDRICH-BLESSING

Fig. 210   *The Amertorp Corporation — Interior*
Chicago, Illinois, 1942
PHOTO: HEDRICH-BLESSING

Fig. 211 *Ford Motor Company*
Willow Run Bomber Plant
Ypsilanti, Michigan, 1943

Fig. 212 *Chrysler Corporation*
Dodge Chicago Plant
Chicago, Illinois, 1943

Fig. 213   *Chrysler Corporation — Machine Shop — Building Number 4*
Dodge Chicago Plant
Chicago, Illinois, 1943
PHOTO: HEDRICH-BLESSING

Fig. 214   *Chrysler Corporation — Airplane Engine Plant — Tool Shop*
Dodge Chicago Plant
Chicago, Illinois, 1943
PHOTO: OWNER

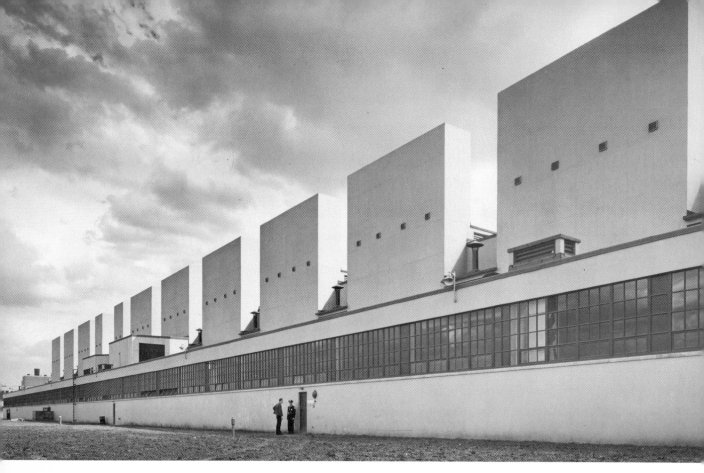

Fig. 215   *Chrysler Corporation — Test Cells, Building Number 5*
Dodge Chicago Plant
Chicago, Illinois, 1943
PHOTO: HEDRICH-BLESSING

Fig. 216   *Chrysler Corporation —
Interior*
Dodge Chicago Plant
Chicago, Illinois, 1943
PHOTO: HEDRICH-BLESSING

ALBERT KAHN ASSOCIATES
1942-1970

by Walter B. Sanders

EXECUTED WORK

Following the death of Albert Kahn in 1942, his brother Louis headed the organization until his own death in 1945. Along with new manufacturing facilities, conversion of and alterations to existing plants to aid in the war effort formed a large part of the firm's work. The roster of commissions in the office reflects the nature of the changes required by an all-out war effort:

Job No. 1509-CK. Converting Boiler Plant from Oil to Coal. Pratt & Whitney Aircraft, East Hartford, Conn.

Job No. 1747-C. Alterations and Additions to Ford Tire Plant to Suit Manufacture and Assembly of Bomber Parts. Ford Motor Company, Dearborn, Mich.

Job No. 1752-AN. Checking Camouflage Nets. Glenn Martin Company, Baltimore County, Md.

Job No. 1915-F. Addition of Women's Lounge in New Manufacturing Building. Curtiss-Wright Corporation, Kenmore, N. Y.

Job No. 1976. Facilities for 105 M.M. Shell Plant. Higgins Plastic Division, Higgins Industries, New Orleans, La.

In the case of new manufacturing facilities, such as the Bomber Plant in Omaha, Nebraska, for the Glenn L. Martin Company, all were generally in the design idiom developed by Albert Kahn.

Fig. 217

George Miehls, a Professional Engineer and product of the Ohio State University, succeeded Louis Kahn. Following cessation of hostilities, the office responded to the tremendous civilian needs of a post-war industry. In its course of professional practice as associates of a large organization, management saw the value of assigning a principal to each project in order to provide the maximum personal attention. This became the normal approach to each project regardless of location. In addition, when a project is located where the registration laws for the practice of architecture and engineering dictate that an individual rather than the corporation be responsible, then the commission is undertaken by a principal. This accounts for the identification of some projects with such principals as George Miehls, Professional Engineer, or Sol King, Architect, and in the case of the Assembly Plant for Ford Motor Company in St. Thomas, Ontario, Canada, the name of Daniel H. Shahan, Professional Engineer. In each instance, however, all the regular technical and professional resources of the firm are utilized.

Fig. 218
Figs. 219, 220   The General Motors Corporation Assembly Plant in Atlanta, Georgia in 1946 was followed by a Ford Motor Company Assembly Plant in St. Louis, Missouri. The technological advances in construction that were developed during World War II are evident in each of these plants. The roofs are flat and unarticulated. Artificial light and mechanical ventilation have in positive fashion eliminated the search for natural light and ventilation expressed in the monitored roofs of many of Albert Kahn's finest works. With small exception, the direction was pointed to the form that large industrial buildings would follow for some years to come.

Fig. 221   One of the exceptions is found in the Printing Plant for R. R. Donnelley & Sons built in Chicago in 1945. Here the functional requirements of the printing process prevailed, and combined with a limited urban site resulted in a multi-story facility pierced with generous windows for natural light and view — in many respects an echo of the Parke-Davis Pharmaceutical Company building erected in Detroit in 1938. The Rotogravure Plant, also for R. R. Donnelley & Sons Company, followed the Printing Plant a few years later in the same vernacular.

In 1948 a group of the younger architects and engineers, who had been with the firm for a decade or more and who had carried major technical responsibilities of the organization during World War II, were taken into the firm's ownership. In time this group, spearheaded by Sol King, a staff architect who had joined the firm in 1935 a year after graduation from the University of Michigan, began to influence the firm's long-range planning in the direction of a renewed emphasis on architectural design and a rekindled interest in institutional and commercial work. Meanwhile, several significant commissions were undertaken by the firm.

Fig. 222   The Jet Engine Plant for Chrysler Corporation built near Detroit in 1951 recalled some of the firm's earlier and highly imaginative treatment of elements of the manufacturing process. The Test Cells in particular have a sculptural quality derived solely from their function. In 1954 the firm associated with Welton Becket & Associates of Los Angeles in providing the Ford Motor Company its new General Office Building for the Ford Division in Dearborn, Michigan. By setting the ground floor level back twelve feet, a covered, weather-protected walkway for employees and visitors was provided, and by means of the cantilevered floor slabs above from which louvres were hung, all-weather sheltering was provided for the continuous band of windows. Landscape Architects for the project were Cornell, Bridgers & Troller of Los Angeles.

Fig. 223

Figs. 224, 225   The same year, work started on the new Undergraduate Library for the University of Michigan in Ann Arbor. This structure, set on a very limited site on the central campus, has proved to be one of the most used of all University facilities. Housing collections of most of the reference works that are required reading in the undergraduate programs, the building is essentially four levels of open-shelf book storage interspersed with informal reading clusters. Artificial lighting and mechanical ventilation are used throughout, and only the north elevation is pierced in any measurable way with windows that provide light and view for subsidiary elements such as the projecting ground floor exhibit space, the audio-visual lab, the two-story multi-purpose room, and a staff lounge.

Fig. 226   Significant non-institutional work undertaken in the mid-1950's includes the Major Supply Depot in Flint, Michigan, for the Chevrolet Motor Division of General Motors Corporation, and the Assembly Plant in St. Louis, Missouri, for

Chrysler Corporation. This latter complex was named one of the nation's "Top Ten Plants" of the year in 1960. The citation from *Modern Manufacturing* (formerly *Factory* Magazine), a McGraw-Hill publication, read "a beautifully balanced manufacturing city (with) a host of excellent plant services giving 'balanced' attention to production, maintenance, and personnel needs." In the Boiler House no effort was made to disguise either its function or the exterior functional elements involved — they became of themselves a part of the total architectural expression. The sloping roof enclosed the interior elements most efficiently and the exterior elements such as the ash silo and the cooling tower on the flat-roofed portion are an integral part of the overall composition.

Fig. 227

Simultaneously, preliminary design studies were started for the Main Office Building of the National Bank of Detroit to be built at the new approach to the Civic Center in Downtown Detroit. The *Architectural Forum* magazine in its February, 1957, issue described the project in the following terms:

Figs. 228, 229

> "The remarkable exterior, among the first in America to be actually executed with staggered windows, rests on a solid line of reasoning. The architects analyzed the bank's upper floor operation as being largely of the big room and bull-pen type, requiring controlled conditions of heat, light and air-conditioning. A wall of only 25% glass would meet the need for view and cut air-conditioning costs.

> "Consequently, the Kahn office's Director of Architecture, Sol King, with Walter Sanders of the University of Michigan as consultant and John Haro as designer, took this practical consideration in hand and developed a building face that would sit pretty in the over-all civic center pattern.

> "With the towers of Detroit's Wall Street area a backdrop, and with the exuberantly Renaissance City Hall as a neighbor, the relatively small bank building had to be visually important, in keeping with its place in the Civic Center. A horizontal or vertical commitment would only call attention to the city hall alongside or the towers overhead. A pattern of holes punched in rigid alignment, the conventional solution in these circumstances, would end up looking foreboding and dingy.

> "The staggered window solution, carefully integrated with the column spacing, yields a simple tapestry that wraps up the building and sets it in place."

The bank building was cited in 1960 for its "excellence of design" by the Detroit Chapter of the American Institute of Architects, and by the American Institute of Steel Construction as "one of the nation's 12 most beautiful steel structures." Design of the major interior spaces was by Ford & Earl Design Associates of Warren, Michigan.

The resurgence of the firm's architectural design capabilities began in 1955. As a Vice President, Sol King set about restructuring the design staff to meet the needs for a broadened base of practice, and one year later was elected Director of Architecture. The resources developed to meet the demands of the emergency decade of World War II and the immediate post-war years served as a platform from which to launch a new and concerted effort to recapture a balance between institutional, commercial, and industrial commissions. In 1955 the author became identified with the firm as Architectural Design Consultant. Shortly after, John

Haro, a graduate in architecture from the University of Michigan and Harvard University, joined the firm as a senior architectural designer. After his arrival the quality of design advanced remarkably, leading to his elevation to Chief Architectural Designer in 1960.

Figs. 230, 231, 232

One of the first industrial type projects to feel the impact of the restructuring was the Jet Engine Maintenance and Overhaul Base for Eastern Air Lines, Inc., in Miami, Florida, for which design started late in 1959. Here the climate with its intense summer heat and sudden showers dictated the minimum number of openings to protect against heat gain and to shelter against driving rains. The light colored metal siding used throughout much of the base assists further in reflecting the heat before it reaches the interiors.

By 1958, when Sol King became president, the firm was well embarked on its new course and there followed a series of distinguished buildings that matched in quality those produced by the firm's founder, Albert Kahn. Receiving either honor awards or citations for the excellence of their design, including the National Bank of Detroit building and the Chrysler Assembly Plant in St. Louis, were eight commercial or institutional structures as well as ten industrial facilities.

Figs. 233, 234, 235

The Parking Structure for the Henry Ford Hospital received local as well as international recognition when it was completed in 1959. The firm received an award for its design from the Detroit Chapter of the American Institute of Architects, and it was cited by the Institute of Civil Engineers of England as "a parking structure of world-wide significance." Commented the *London Observer* of November 27, 1960, "The parking problem is solved with grace, economy, and efficiency in this four-story garage designed by Albert Kahn Associates of Detroit." The sculptural grilles marked a radical departure from past exterior treatment of open-deck parking structures when it was introduced. The compound-curved panels of precast white concrete not only screen the vehicular activity within but provide a setting appropriate to the institution's residential neighborhood.

Figs. 236, 237, 238, 239

The Physics & Astronomy Building, erected in Ann Arbor in 1962 for the University of Michigan, received awards from both the Detroit Chapter of the American Institute of Architects and the Michigan Society of Architects. In describing the complex the *Architectural Record* of April, 1964, noted, "this arrangement of two buildings—one high, the other low and spreading—offers a neat solution to the common problem of adding density to a campus without giving it an overcrowded look. The bold, continuous precast band at the second floor level and the stepping back of the walls under this bank serve to create a strong horizontality that ties both buildings together and gives the entire complex fine scale." Landscaping for the project was by Johnson, Johnson & Roy of Ann Arbor, Michigan.

Fig. 240

The Truck Assembly Plant at Springfield, Ohio, erected in 1966 for the International Harvester Company, consists of high concrete panels on the lower portion of the factory wall treated in a manner to add interest to the surface. To provide contrast a white quartz aggregate was used for the fascia panels of the office wing at the front of the plant. The entire complex is unified by the use of colored metal siding on the upper walls which complements the other materials. Selected from an original list of over 1500 new manufacturing facilities completed in 1966, the plant was cited by *Modern Manufacturing* (formerly *Factory* Magazine), a McGraw-Hill publication, for its "outstanding interest and significance to a broad range of operating executives in many types of manufacturing industries and in companies of all sizes." Judging was based on "overall excellence in planning and construction."

Another award-winning structure was the Air Terminal Building for the City of Detroit. Although termed "controversial" by the jury for the competition conducted by the Detroit Chapter of the American Institute of Architects, the jury praised the building for its use of materials. Dull black porcelain-enamel panels, which run the length of the building and over the entrance, are a feature of the design. The panels and gray glass windows located below them slope outward above the exposed concrete around the perimeter of the building, helping to reduce glare and solar heat gain. On this project Ford & Earl Design Associates of Warren, Michigan, were responsible for the interiors.

Fig. 241

In 1965 the firm was commissioned by Avon Products, Inc., to design a new Laboratory and Office Building to be erected at Springdale, Ohio, which would provide a "cheerful, efficient, and attractive environment for the company's employees . . . and portray its sense of responsibility to the host community by reflecting the warmth and friendliness associated with the company's sales representatives." How well these goals were met is expressed in the jury comment in connection with one of the two architectural awards received by the office for the design of this manufacturing, sales and distribution center. The comment reads: "To relate successfully the diverse functions of large factory warehouse space to the smaller, more intimate requirements of office and administration is a difficult architectural problem resolved in this case with skill and sensitivity. The jury particularly commends the continuity of forms, the control and creation of a variety of exterior spaces, the success in breaking down the volume contrast between required manufacturing and office space, the concern for providing a pleasant working environment in and around the building, and the general consistency of architectural development." The strong emphasis on the horizontal features of the complex was developed to achieve human scale as well as a sense of shelter and earth-bound quality. In addition, because of the generous use of glass, protection was desirable against extremes of solar exposure. In contrast to the simple horizontal projections of the roof over the office area are the sloped metal roof fascias used over the manufacturing and shipping area, the employees dining and meeting room, and the public entrance canopy. For this project Braun & Chamberlin, Inc. of Orange, New Jersey handled the interiors, and Johnson, Johnson & Roy of Ann Arbor, Michigan, the landscaping.

Figs. 242, 243, 244, 245

The Southeastern Branch Facilities at Atlanta, Georgia, also for Avon Products, Inc., was completed late in 1969. The owner's "desire to provide a pleasant environment for its employees and visitors" led to many amenities unusual for a warehouse and order-processing center. "The site was chosen for its potential to provide enjoyable views to the outside. Existing natural foliage was retained wherever possible and was augmented by landscaping. A man-made lake with a water jet is the focal point of an outdoor area developed for employee use, and two pools flank the skylighted lobby pavilion. Large window areas take full advantage of these natural surroundings." The above are the comments applying to this award-winning entry in the Michigan Society of Architects' 1970 Honor Awards Program. Another significant honor for the design of the facility was conferred by the Atlanta Civic Design Commission. Their award to the owner read: "For dedicated service in the development of environmental

Figs. 246, 247, 248, 249

excellence." Contributing to this excellence were Ray Lang, Inc. of Atlanta for the interiors, Edward L. Daugherty, also of Atlanta, for the landscaping, and Betty Jacob of Detroit, sculptress.

Figs. 250, 251, 252, 253

The Administrative Office Building erected in 1968 in Saginaw, Michigan, for the Chevrolet-Saginaw Foundries Division of General Motors Corporation, houses management, personnel, accounting, purchasing and engineering functions for an adjacent foundry complex. Winner of four awards since its completion, the last honor for the design of this building was conferred by the Detroit Chapter of the American Institute of Architects. By elevating the building above the ground, covered employee parking was provided as well as a more dramatic setting on a site located below the main highway. Earth banks screen all parked cars from view, and a ten-foot roof overhang provides sun control and minimizes dirt accumulation on the windows. The exterior columns of weathering steel, separated from the building, allow uninterrupted expanses of glass and make fire-proofing unnecessary. Thus exposed they serve to strengthen the structural expression of the building.

Fig. 254

Representing a departure from the norm in manufacturing circles is the Administrative Headquarters Building designed in 1965 for The Trane Company of La Crosse, Wisconsin. Instead of locating their new administrative center adjacent to existing manufacturing facilities, the company elected to locate in an undeveloped area adjacent to the city where a park-like environment could be realized. The 40-acre site lies in a generally residential area at the foot of ruggedly sloping hills and stony bluffs. A feature of the landscaping treatment is the pool at the main entrance to the building. Fed from a nearby well, the pool includes an illuminated fountain and serves as a reservoir for sprinkling the landscaped area. The structure of reinforced concrete frame is designed for the addition of one floor over the entire building. Set on a black granite base, white marble is used for facing the exterior structural members to provide contrast with the gray window glass. Interiors were by Ford & Earl Design Associates, and landscaping by Eichstedt, Grissim, Young & Associates, of Detroit.

Fig. 255

The R. R. Donnelley & Sons Company Corporate Office Building in Chicago varies considerably from the administrative headquarters for The Trane Company. In this instance the proximity of several printing facilities buildings, all owned by the same company and all clad in brick with stone and terra cotta trim used for the arched windows, was decisive in arriving at the solution. Besides using the same brick to strengthen the visual relationship of the new building with those existing, precast, aggregate surfaced concrete units were used to frame the openings and recall the trim used elsewhere. The arched window frame units contribute a further visual tie with the old buildings, and add a graceful curving line to contrast with the otherwise rectilinear character of the new building. The deep window reveals were conceived as light cutoffs for the southeast to southwest range of the sun and, together with the gray window glass, serve to keep heat and light penetration within reasonable limits. In addition, the deep reveals lend a three-dimensional, sculptural effect and serve to enrich the surface with an ever-changing pattern of light and shade.

Over the years a host of institutional facilities, beginning with the original building for Children's Hospital in Detroit in 1896, were designed by Albert Kahn and his successors. The University of Michigan alone accounts for 33 structures beginning with the Engineering Building erected in 1903. Several, not including the Undergraduate Library and the Physics & Astronomy Building at the University of Michigan, are among recent projects undertaken by the present firm.

The Life Sciences Research Center Building, providing laboratories and offices for teaching and research in the fields of biology and chemistry, was completed in 1961 for Wayne State University in Detroit. In keeping with its urban setting, the building is set back at the ground level to form an arcade which serves as a covered passageway and sheltered congregating space. The open circulation serves to connect the new building with the University's existing Science Hall to the east. The buildings are also connected at the second and third floor levels by a glass-enclosed bridge. The master plan of the campus, the teaching and research functions and especially the mechanical requirements represented major determinants in arriving at the final design. No air is recirculated because of the fumes and the possibility of contamination. To provide the immense volume of fresh air required, four six-foot-diameter fresh air intake stacks or nostrils at the front of the building were used. Capped with mushroom-like aluminum shields, air is drawn in, conditioned and distributed throughout the building and finally discharged by a battery of exhaust fans located behind the penthouse screen. The materials and finishes were selected with the view of providing planar differentiation and value contrast. Structural elements such as the columns, beams and slabs are of smooth, poured-in-place concrete with a white cement finish. The precast concrete wall panels are faced with a white quartz aggregate and provide a textural contrast with the framing members. Windows are of gray glass to minimize heat gain and to accentuate the unbroken lines of the columns.

Fig. 256

The Synagogue Center for Congregation Shaarey Zedek in Southfield, Michigan, completed in 1963, was a project in association with Percival Goodman, Architect, of New York City. Noted for his design of ecclesiastical buildings, Goodman was primarily responsible for design and the Kahn Associates for the working drawings and all engineering and mechanical aspects. In his impressive work, "The Buildings of Detroit," published by Wayne State University, W. Hawkins Ferry refers to the influence of Frank Lloyd Wright's ideas on the design of the synagogue: "The Wrightian formula has found monumental expression in the Congregation Shaarey Zedek Synagogue in Southfield. The sanctuary juts out like a giant Hebrew tabernacle or tent on a bluff overlooking Northwestern Highway. Stained glass windows symbolizing the burning bush follow the slope of the roof. On the interior of the sanctuary is a 40-foot marble ark of the scrolls." Bold and forceful in its expression, the sanctuary, designed to accommodate a congregation of 1200, may be expanded for the High Holy Days to seat 3600 people. Containing, besides the sanctuary and its two flanking social halls, spacious lobby and foyer areas, five chapels, a library, classrooms, meeting and craft rooms, the building reflects the multi-use requirements of a modern synagogue center. Many artists contributed their talents to various parts of the building. Jan Peter Stern was responsible for the exterior sculptured pylon behind the Ark which symbolically represents Mount Sinai with ten figures representing the Decalogue inscribed on it, and Robert Pinart designed the stained glass panels that frame the marble Ark. Thomas McClure was the sculptor of the ten metal Hebrew letters applied to the Ark and that symbolize the ten commandments. Interior design was by Naomi Goodman of New York City; landscaping by Eichstedt, Grissim, Young

Figs. 257, 258

& Associates of Detroit; and acoustical consulting by Bolt, Beranek & Newman, Inc. of Cambridge, Massachusetts.

Figs. 259, 260 Two other institutional buildings by the firm are the Natural Resources Building and the Food Science Research Building, both completed in 1969, for Michigan State University in East Lansing, Michigan. Each had essentially the same requirements — research laboratories, classrooms, and offices — and the structural framing and finishes are generally the same. The structural system is characterized by the use of full-height precast concrete columns along the front and back that have beams at each floor level reaching out half way to connect with the adjacent beams and columns. To these "tree" columns contrasting lime-stone panels are added to form the major exterior finish except for the end walls which are of brick. Located across a campus drive from each other, the buildings combine to provide a sense of unity to the immediate area.

Figs. 261, 262 Planned to blend in with the residential area which surrounds it, the Jewish Home for the Aged in Detroit was completed in 1965. The facility consists of three basic elements: a 3-story residential structure with a special wing providing full hospital services; a single story element containing central facilities such as administration, meeting hall, kitchen and dining rooms; and another single story motel type unit for guests or temporary residents. The varying height of the elements, as well as the contrasting roof forms and spread-out nature of the complex, contribute much to the non-institutional character of the Home. Eichstedt, Grissim, Young & Associates were Landscape Architects.

Fig. 263 Within the medical classification of institutional buildings, the Radiotherapy Building completed in 1968 is part of a complex of structures designed by the firm over a 20-year period for the Sinai Hospital of Detroit. The building houses a two-million-volt cobalt treatment unit, a 250,000-volt deep X-ray therapy unit, and facilities for a 40-million-volt betatron unit in below-ground-level chambers shielded by ultra-high-density concrete. The form of the building derives from the expression of the semi-circular patients ramp leading to the below-grade facilities, above which are located a film storage unit and conference room. The applied sculpture above the ramp form is the work of Arthur Schneider.

Figs. 264, 265 Also a part of the Sinai Hospital complex is the Auditorium and Conference Center constructed almost simultaneously with the Radiotherapy Building. Located so as to provide direct access from the street, the Center is connected to the main hospital at both of its two levels. The main floor provides for a generous entrance and display gallery from which two conference rooms and a 265-seat auditorium are accessible. Under the auditorium is an expansion of the existing hospital cafeteria.

The building takes advantage of the sloping site in a way to provide full height windows along one side of the cafeteria. A unifying element in the design is the expression of the gallery that links the two major elements and terminates at each end with a forceful concrete canopy. The interiors were the work of Walter Duncan of Detroit, and the landscaping by Eichstedt, Grissim, Young & Associates.

Fig. 266 With the exception of works in progress, the C. S. Mott Children's Hospital at the University of Michigan in Ann Arbor is the latest medical facility to be designed by the firm. This unit of the University Medical Center serves as a regional hospital treating serious and long-term child illnesses as well as providing a teaching laboratory for student nurses and doctors. Present day approaches to the treatment of childhood illnesses made particularly important the inclusion of ample space for recreation and continued classroom instruction. These are accommodated at the roof level above the four patient floors. The ground floor is devoted primarily to administrative and medical services. A feature of the design which adds interest to the total concept is the paired cellular-like, projecting bathrooms along both long sides of the patient floors. The exterior treatment is concrete for the exposed framing members with walls of brick matching the adjacent Out-Patients Building and Maternity Hospital.

Several industrial plants also comprise recent works of the firm. Of these at least four deserve special mention. The Stamping Plant at Woodhaven, Michigan, *Figs. 267, 268* for the Ford Motor Company was a massive undertaking that required a "crash" program involving a degree of cooperation among owner, architect, and contractor seldom achieved in the construction industry. Ten months after the firm made the first preliminary drawing, production started in part of this 2.5 million square foot building. In an article published in January, 1967, *Architectural Record* commented "The design of this Ford Stamping Plant has an ordered simplicity and clean strength entirely suitable for such expansive, large-scale industrial projects — surely an element in bettering worker morale and productivity. In addition to performing its role as a manufacturing facility, this vast building provides many special facilities and amenities for its 4000 employees." One particular amenity worth noting is the means by which employees enter the building — from the parking lot a moving stairway carries them to a bridge spanning a heavily used driveway, to arrive safely and conveniently on a mezzanine housing locker and shower rooms. The design of the major interior spaces in the administrative wing was by Ford & Earl Design Associates, and the landscaping by Eichstedt, Grissim, Young & Associates.

A significant innovation in the industrial production process is found in the Assembly Plant at St. Thomas, Ontario, Canada, for the Ford Motor Company. *Figs. 269, 270* Completed in 1968, here a completely automated 10-story "selectivity tower" stores up to 40 cars before delivering them to the final trim assembly lines. By providing a vertical loop in the assembly process, precious ground level space was conserved for other operations. During the early design phases another and taller tower was considered for the storage of car bodies which were to be selected as needed to meet the matching chassis at the point of their assembly. Here, a half-century after Henry Ford conceived the continuously moving assembly line (Fig. 34), we find one of the first significant variations in the process. Landscape Architects for the project were Sasaki, Strong & Associates, Ltd., of Toronto.

The Van Dyke Plant for the Transmission and Chassis Division of Ford *Fig. 271* Motor Company is the second facility for the Ford Motor Company to be erected in Sterling Heights, Michigan in recent years. Exterior materials are color-coated aluminum siding above a sill wall of precast exposed-aggregate concrete. Similar materials are used on the 2-story office building to strengthen the relationship between the factory and office. Ford & Earl Design Associates were responsible for the interiors of the major spaces in the office wing, and Johnson, Johnson & Roy of Ann Arbor were the Landscape Architects.

The final example of recent industrial architecture by the firm deserving of special mention is the Die and Engineering Center for the Chevrolet-Flint Manu- *Fig. 272* facturing Division of General Motors Corporation in Flint, Michigan. This modest size but highly specialized facility contains two crane bays with a 3-story core area between. The core houses offices, a cafeteria, apprentice and pattern shop, a heat treat area, and employee facilities as well as a fully-carpeted engineering section of more than an acre. With a slope of 14 feet from front to rear, the site dictated locating the first floor level at the lower level for ease of shipping and receiving, also for easy employee entrance from the parking lot.

Building columns are of exposed structural steel, and exterior walls are of light gray color-coated insulated aluminum siding from the top of the concrete at the lower level to the underside of the black anodized aluminum sash. The sash are placed approximately 12 inches in front of the lower portion of the wall. At the ends and mid-points where cross bracing of the wall is required, the siding is of medium gray and is located directly behind the front face of the exposed columns. Above the sash and enclosing the columns is a band of black color-coated aluminum siding. Accents are given the structure at the main and employee entrances through the use of black canopies. A photo of the roof detail shows the setbacks at the sash and walls.

Fig. 273

Named by the American Institute of Steel Construction as one of the nation's twelve most beautiful steel buildings erected in 1969 is the Power and Generating Facility designed for the City of Traverse City, Michigan. The jurors' comments read: "This is a fine example of clear, functional design. The form of the building reflects the location of the complex equipment within. The result is a simplicity of design that is difficult to achieve." The walls of the structure are blue-gray baked enamel on aluminum above a base of face brick that matches the adjoining existing building.

Fig. 274

With a long history in the design of large hangars reaching back through World Wars I and II, the firm was well equipped to cope with the problems posed by the huge United Air Lines Maintenance Hangar at O'Hare International Airport in Chicago. The structure consists of two main hangar areas, each 225 feet wide with an 80-foot wide six-story office shop-storage core between the two hangar sections. Each hangar space houses major maintenance and cleaning activities in a column-free area capable of accommodating a single jumbo jet or four Boeing 727's or four Douglas DC-8's. A feature of the design is the twelve canopy type doors that permit straight through maneuverability of the aircraft — three for the front and rear of each hangar. Ten of the doors are 51-feet high and the two center doors swing up to provide a clear opening of 73-feet to permit clearance of the 65-foot high tail of the Boeing 747. Computers were used extensively in calculating the intricate wind stresses and in establishing the most efficient construction schedule. The exterior walls are of colored metal siding above a base of precast concrete panels.

Figs. 275, 276

WORK IN PROGRESS

Separate from the impressive works executed by the firm since the death of its founder is a series of projects presently in either the design or construction stage. One of these, the Hospital and Parking Structure for the Children's Hospital of Michigan in Detroit, goes back to 1964 when the first submission of schematic plans was made. Now nearly complete, the hospital will serve as the

Fig. 277

pediatrics center of the Detroit Medical Center located on an urban renewal site of some 250 acres of land.

The lower two floors of the building house all patient and staff central facilities, with the upper four floors being devoted solely to patients. The patient floors are in the form of an "H" with the nursing units housed in the elements flanking the core services. The 320-bed facility is enclosed by an exposed concrete frame in-filled with face brick and aluminum and glass panels. The 500-car parking structure is attached to the hospital and opened for use in the summer of 1969.

Of two new buildings designed by the present firm and now under construction for the University of Michigan in Ann Arbor, the Harlan Hatcher Graduate Library is the most advanced. Named to honor President-Emeritus Harlan Hatcher, the building consists of an open arcade first floor, seven floors housing 830,000 volumes and 532 student and faculty carrels, and is topped with a mechanical equipment penthouse. Located directly south of the General Library, designed by Albert Kahn in 1919 (Fig. 72), and north and behind the Clements Library, also designed by Kahn in 1922 (Fig. 134), the main building block is a column-free space of approximately 275 feet by 50 feet at each level. Stairs and utility cores are contained in separate adjoining towers and provide a connection to the General Library on the second floor. A cross-campus walkway runs the full length of the open ground floor space, flanked by a small landscaped plaza between the arcade and Clements Library. Johnson, Johnson & Roy are the Landscape Architects for the project and responsible for the design of the plaza.

Figs. 278, 279

Sharing a relationship similar to that of the new Library is the Classroom and Office Building scheduled for completion in about a year. This building completes a city-block composition that includes Hill Auditorium (Fig. 63) and the Burton Memorial Tower designed by Albert Kahn in 1914 and 1936 respectively. The first floor contains two auditoriums and two large lecture halls with easy access to all from entrances at the four corners of the building. Seminar rooms and a language laboratory occupy the second floor, with faculty offices located in the upper two floors. Brick facing of the building will provide a visual relationship with Hill Auditorium and at the same time provide contrast to the vertical limestone shaft of Burton Tower.

Fig. 280

One of the largest projects ever undertaken by either the founding firm or its successor is Appliance Park — East, for General Electric Company in the "new-town" of Columbia, Maryland. This major G.E. industrial facility is taking form on an attractive 1100 acre site situated midway between Washington and Baltimore in a region characterized by rolling topography. In arriving at the master plan for the project the natural character and beauty of the site were preserved without impingement on the manufacturing requirements. Sensitive relationship to the immediate neighboring areas is also respected by retaining a natural buffer around the periphery of the site, broken only as necessary for vehicular and railway access. The large volume of plant traffic entering the site from the new divided highways which form the boundaries on three sides, requires the use of three clover-leaf interchanges to assure smooth traffic flow. The on-site roadway system, containing 14 miles of roadway, has separate networks for employee and truck traffic.

Fig. 281

Due to the tremendous areas of roofs and pavements, on an 1100 acre site that varies approximately 140 feet in elevation over a rolling terrain, elaborate provisions were necessary to prevent downstream flooding from the rapid runoff of storm water. These provisions include an 85-million-gallon water retention basin from which the storm water can be released at a low rate of flow.

Relative to the production processes, the movement of raw material is from the peripheral end of the manufacturing buildings to the opposite end facing the central mall. Here it is carried by overhead conveyor to the warehouse for shipment or storage. Because of the relationship of administrative facilities to the flow of products, as well as the opportunity to take advantage of the wooded mall, the office buildings are located on the mall side of the manufacturing buildings with the product conveyor enclosures passing overhead. This allows the employee cafeterias and the offices to overlook the park-like mall.

Fig. 282

Figs. 283, 284

Eight appliance manufacturing buildings, a large central warehouse, and twenty auxiliary buildings will eventually occupy the site. Range Building No. 1, comprised of over one million square feet, is under construction as is the Warehouse of equivalent size and the Air Conditioning Building. Johnson, Johnson & Roy of Ann Arbor served as Landscape Architects. Jackson and Moreland of Boston served as Mechanical Engineering Consultants.

Fig. 285

Ground was broken in April this year for a nine-story Newspaper Publishing Building for the *Washington Post* in Washington, D.C. The new building, plus modernization and additions to existing facilities, will double the size of the present establishment. The original building into which the *Post* moved in 1950 as well as the large addition completed in 1960 are also the work of the present firm. The facade of the new building, of light colored face brick, will set back slightly at each floor level to provide interest in an otherwise simple plane. The large windows will also be successively recessed, producing increasing planar relief and differentiation at each floor level. The Detroit firm of Ford and Earl Design Associates has been commissioned to undertake the design of the interiors.

Fig. 286

Completed only last April was the Service Parts Processing Redistribution Center for the Ford Motor Company in Brownstown Township, Michigan. The largest single roof structure ever designed by Albert Kahn Associates is also the largest single facility ever commissioned by the Ford Motor Company. The 3-million square foot center is large enough to cover 62 football fields. Essentially a warehouse, the building has a minimum of openings except in the office extension. The walls consist of dark colored asbestos and metal siding above a natural colored concrete base. Eichstedt, Grissim, Young & Associates are Landscape Architects for the project.

Figs. 287, 288

Design studies for the Office Building and Parking Structure for the Fisher-New Center Company were started in 1967. To be located across the street from the General Motors Building and the Fisher Building, the proposed structure would occupy one of the few remaining premium sites in the city. Designed as a rental office building, the structure would also include parking for tenants in an adjoining building, and be connected at the concourse level with both the General Motors and the Fisher Building. The simple, direct form of the 30-story shaft would about equal the height of the Fisher Building across Second Avenue to the west.

As is true of the Albert Kahn period, the projects of those who succeeded him and form a part of this exhibit are but a sample of a much larger total. Those selected have been primarily on the basis of their appeal to a non-professional audience of viewers. Of Kahn's successors the one most like him in background is Sol King, the present leader of the firm. He was born abroad, came to this country at an early age, worked as an apprentice under one whom he admired, and has spent almost all his professional career with the firm. As was Kahn, he is immersed in all aspects of architecture and is a respected and able leader. Yet, he is a warm, sympathetic individual generous to all who seek his help.

Without the perspective of time any critical evaluation of the firm's work since the death of its founder would be superficial. It can be said with some confidence, nevertheless, that the firm is continuing to fulfill the aspirations of Albert Kahn to whom this occasion is dedicated.

X. Completed Work
Albert Kahn Associates 1942-1970

Fig. 217   *Glenn L. Martin Company*
Bomber Plant
Omaha, Nebraska, 1943
PHOTO: HEDRICH-BLESSING

Fig. 218 *General Motors Corporation*
Assembly Plant
Atlanta, Georgia, 1946
PHOTO: GM PHOTOGRAPHIC

Fig. 219 *Ford Motor Company*
Lincoln-Mercury Division, Assembly Plant
St. Louis, Missouri, 1947
PHOTO: HEDRICH-BLESSING

Fig. 220 *Ford Motor Company*
Lincoln-Mercury Division, Assembly Plant—Night View
St. Louis, Missouri, 1947
PHOTO: HEDRICH-BLESSING

Fig. 221   *R. R. Donnelley & Sons Company*
Printing Plant
Chicago, Illinois, 1945
PHOTO: HEDRICH-BLESSING

Fig. 222   *Chrysler Corporation*
Jet Engine Plant, Test Cells
Macomb County, Michigan, 1951
PHOTO: HEDRICH-BLESSING

Fig. 223 *Ford Motor Company*
Ford Division, General Office Building
Welton Becket & Associates and Albert Kahn Associates
Dearborn, Michigan, 1954
PHOTO: HEDRICH-BLESSING

Fig. 224 *University of Michigan*
Undergraduate Library
Ann Arbor, Michigan, 1956
PHOTO: HEDRICH-BLESSING

Fig. 225   *University of Michigan*
Undergraduate Library, Entrance Detail
Ann Arbor, Michigan, 1956
PHOTO: HEDRICH-BLESSING

Fig. 226   *General Motors Corporation*
Chevrolet Motor Division, Major Supply Depot
Flint, Michigan, 1956
PHOTO: HEDRICH-BLESSING

Fig. 227   *Chrysler Corporation*
Passenger Car Assembly Plant, Boiler House
St. Louis, Missouri, 1956
PHOTO: HEDRICH-BLESSING

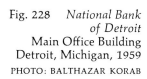

Fig. 228   *National Bank
of Detroit*
Main Office Building
Detroit, Michigan, 1959
PHOTO: BALTHAZAR KORAB

Fig. 229 *National Bank of Detroit*
Main Office Building, Woodward Avenue Entrance
Detroit, Michigan, 1959
PHOTO: BALTHAZAR KORAB

Fig. 230 *Eastern Air Lines*
Jet Engine Maintenance and Overhaul Base
George H. Miehls, Professional Engineer, and Albert Kahn Associates
Miami, Florida, 1959-60
PHOTO: BLACK-BAKER

Fig. 231   *Eastern Air Lines*
Jet Engine Maintenance and Overhaul Base, Test Cells
George H. Miehls, Professional Engineer, and Albert Kahn Associates
Miami, Florida, 1959-60
PHOTO: BLACK-BAKER

Fig. 232   *Eastern Air Lines*
Jet Engine Maintenance and Overhaul Base, Hangar
George H. Miehls, Professional Engineer, and Albert Kahn Associates
Miami, Florida, 1959-60
PHOTO: LAWRENCE S. WILLIAMS

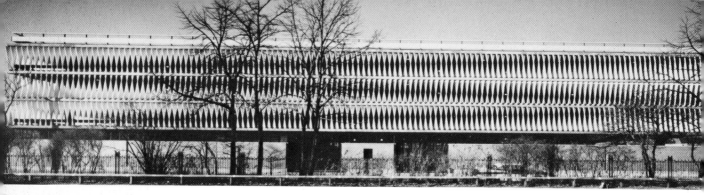

Fig. 233 *Henry Ford Hospital*
Parking Structure
Detroit, Michigan, 1959
PHOTO: DANIEL BARTUSH

Fig. 234 *Henry Ford Hospital*
Parking Structure,
Detail of Panels
Detroit, Michigan, 1959
PHOTO: J. NACHBAR

Fig. 235 *Henry Ford Hospital*
General Services & Parking Building
Detroit, Michigan, 1967
PHOTO: LENS ART

Fig. 236 *University of Michigan*
Physics and Astronomy Building, General View
Ann Arbor, Michigan, 1963
PHOTO: DANIEL BARTUSH

Fig. 237 *University of Michigan*
Physics and Astronomy Building, View of Lecture Halls
Ann Arbor, Michigan, 1963
PHOTO: BALTHAZAR KORAB

Fig. 238 *University of Michigan*
Physics and Astronomy Building
East Elevation
Ann Arbor, Michigan, 1963
PHOTO: BALTHAZAR KORAB

Fig. 239 *University of Michigan*
Physics and Astronomy Building,
Connecting Bridge
Ann Arbor, Michigan, 1963
PHOTO: LENS ART

Fig. 240 *International Harvester Company*
Motor Division, Truck Assembly Plant
Sol King, F.A.I.A., and Albert Kahn Associates
Springfield, Ohio, 1966
PHOTO: GEORGE STILLE

Fig. 241 *City of Detroit*
Air Terminal Building
Detroit, Michigan, 1966
PHOTO: LENS ART

Fig. 242 *Avon Products, Inc.*
Laboratory and Office Building
Sol King, F.A.I.A., and Albert Kahn Associates
Springdale, Ohio, 1965
PHOTO: BALTHAZAR KORAB

Fig. 243   *Avon Products, Inc.*
Laboratory and Office Building, Employee Patio
Sol King, F.A.I.A., and Albert Kahn Associates
Springdale, Ohio, 1965
PHOTO: BALTHAZAR KORAB

Fig. 244   *Avon Products, Inc.*
Laboratory and Office Building, Packaging Area
Sol King, F.A.I.A., and Albert Kahn Associates
Springdale, Ohio, 1965
PHOTO: BALTHAZAR KORAB

Fig. 245   *Avon Products, Inc.*
Laboratory and Office Building, Entrance Canopy
Sol King, F.A.I.A., and Albert Kahn Associates
Springdale, Ohio, 1965
PHOTO: BALTHAZAR KORAB

Fig. 246   *Avon Products, Inc.*
Southeastern Branch Facilities
Sol King, F.A.I.A., and Albert Kahn Associates
Atlanta, Georgia, 1969
PHOTO: BRYAN-YOUNG

Fig. 247   *Avon Products, Inc.*
Southeastern Branch Facilities, Public Entrance
Sol King, F.A.I.A., and Albert Kahn Associates
Atlanta, Georgia, 1969
PHOTO: BRYAN-YOUNG

Fig. 248   *Avon Products, Inc.*
Southeastern Branch Facilities, Employee Entrance
Sol King, F.A.I.A., and Albert Kahn Associates
Atlanta, Georgia, 1969
PHOTO: BRYAN-YOUNG

Fig. 250   *General Motors Corporation*
Chevrolet-Saginaw Grey Iron Foundry Division
Administrative Office Building
Saginaw, Michigan, 1968
PHOTO: DANIEL BARTUSH

Fig. 251   *General Motors Corporation*
Chevrolet-Saginaw Grey Iron Foundry Division
Administrative Office Building, South Elevation
Saginaw, Michigan, 1968
PHOTO: DANIEL BARTUSH

Fig. 252   *General Motors Corporation*
Chevrolet-Saginaw Grey Iron Foundry Division
Administrative Office Building, Main Entrance Pavilion
—Exterior Stair Detail
Saginaw, Michigan, 1968
PHOTO: DANIEL BARTUSH

Fig. 253   *General Motors Corporation*
Chevrolet-Saginaw Grey Iron Foundry Division
Administrative Office Building, Exterior Detail
Saginaw, Michigan, 1968
PHOTO: DANIEL BARTUSH

Fig. 254   *The Trane Company*
Administration Building, Main Entrance Facade
Sol King, F.A.I.A., and Albert Kahn Associates
La Crosse, Wisconsin, 1967
PHOTO: HEDRICH-BLESSING

Fig. 255   *R. R. Donnelley & Sons Company*
Corporate Office Building
Chicago, Illinois, 1961
PHOTO: HEDRICH-BLESSING

Fig. 256   *Wayne State University*
Life Sciences Research Center Building
Walter B. Sanders, F.A.I.A., Design Consultant, and Albert Kahn Associates
Detroit, Michigan, 1961

PHOTO: BALTHAZAR KORAB

Fig. 257   *Congregation Shaarey Zedek*
Synagogue Center, East Elevation
Percival Goodman, F.A.I.A., New York City, and Albert Kahn Associates
Southfield, Michigan, 1962
PHOTO: BALTHAZAR KORAB

Fig. 258   *Congregation Shaarey Zedek*
Synagogue, Sanctuary
Percival Goodman, F.A.I.A., New York City, and Albert Kahn Associates
Southfield, Michigan, 1962
PHOTO: BALTHAZAR KORAB

Fig. 259 *Michigan State University*
Natural Resources Building
East Lansing, Michigan, 1967
PHOTO: ARCHITECTURAL ARTS

Fig. 260 *Michigan State University*
Food Science Building
East Lansing, Michigan, 1967
PHOTO: ARCHITECTURAL ARTS

Fig. 261 *Jewish Home For Aged*
East Elevation
Detroit, Michigan, 1966
PHOTO: LENS ART

Fig. 262 *Jewish Home For Aged*
South Elevation of Main Entrance
Detroit, Michigan, 1966
PHOTO: LENS ART

Fig. 263 *Sinai Hospital*
Radiotherapy Building
Detroit, Michigan, 1968
PHOTO: LENS ART

Fig. 264 *Sinai Hospital*
Auditorium and Conference Center, Main Entrance
Detroit, Michigan, 1968
PHOTO: LENS ART

Fig. 265 *Sinai Hospital*
Auditorium and Conference Center, West Elevation
Detroit, Michigan, 1968
PHOTO: LENS ART

Fig. 266   *University of Michigan*
C. S. Mott Children's Hospital
Ann Arbor, Michigan, 1969
PHOTO: BOULEVARD PHOTOGRAPHIC, INC.

Fig. 267   *Ford Motor Company*
Stamping Plant
Woodhaven, Michigan, 1966
PHOTO: LENS ART

Fig. 268 *Ford Motor Company*
Stamping Plant, Administration Building
Woodhaven, Michigan, 1966
PHOTO: LENS ART

Fig. 269 *Ford Motor Company*
Automotive Assembly Plant
Daniel H. Shahan, Professional Engineer, and Albert Kahn Associates
St. Thomas, Ontario, Canada, 1968
PHOTO: DANIEL BARTUSH

Fig. 270 *Ford Motor Company*
Automotive Assembly Plant, View of Selectivity Tower
Daniel H. Shahan, Professional Engineer, and Albert Kahn Associates
St. Thomas, Ontario, Canada, 1968
PHOTO: DANIEL BARTUSH

Fig. 271 *Ford Motor Company*
Transmission and Chassis Division
Van Dyke Plant
Sterling Heights, Michigan, 1969
PHOTO: LENS ART

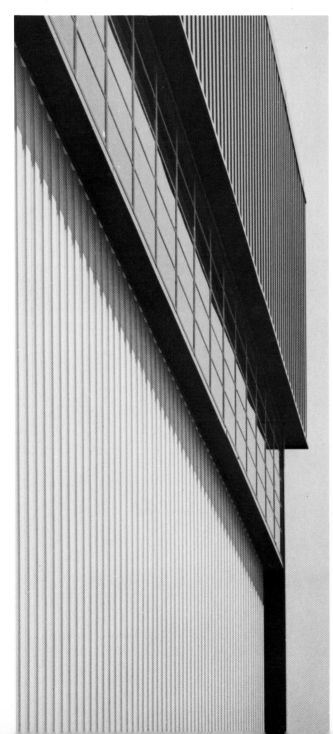

Fig. 272 *General Motors Corporation*
Chevrolet-Flint Manufacturing Division
Die and Engineering Center
Flint, Michigan, 1968
PHOTO: DANIEL BARTUSH

Fig. 273 *General Motors Corporation*
Chevrolet-Flint Manufacturing Division
Die and Engineering Center, Exterior Detail
Flint, Michigan, 1968
PHOTO: DANIEL BARTUSH

Fig. 274   *Traverse City*
Power and Generating Facilities
Alterations and Additions
Traverse City, Michigan, 1969
PHOTO: HEDRICH-BLESSING

Fig. 275   *United Air Lines*
Major Maintenance Hangar, West Hangar
O'Hare International Airport
Chicago, Illinois, 1968
PHOTO: HEDRICH-BLESSING

Fig. 276   *United Air Lines*
Major Maintenance Hangar, East Hangar
O'Hare International Airport
Chicago, Illinois, 1968
PHOTO: HEDRICH-BLESSING

XI. Work In Progress
Albert Kahn Associates

All photographs in this section are of renderings or models

Fig. 277 *Children's Hospital of Michigan*
Hospital and Parking Structure
Detroit, Michigan
PHOTO: LENS ART

Fig. 278 *University of Michigan*
Central Campus (Harlan Hatcher) Library
Ann Arbor, Michigan
PHOTO: DANIEL BARTUSH

Fig. 279 *University of Michigan*
Central Campus (Harlan Hatcher) Library
Ann Arbor, Michigan
PHOTO: NATIONAL REPRODUCTIONS

1914   1937   1970

Fig. 280 *University of Michigan*
Classroom and Office Building
Ann Arbor, Michigan
PHOTO: NATIONAL REPRODUCTIONS

Fig. 281 *General Electric Company*
Appliance Park-East
Sol King, F.A.I.A., and Albert Kahn Associates
Columbia, Maryland
PHOTO: DANIEL BARTUSH

Fig. 282   *General Electric Company*
Appliance Park-East, Range Building No. 1
Sol King, F.A.I.A., and Albert Kahn Associates
Columbia, Maryland

PHOTO: NATIONAL REPRODUCTIONS

Fig. 283   *General Electric Company*
Appliance Park-East, Warehouse
Sol King, F.A.I.A., and Albert Kahn Associates
Columbia, Maryland

PHOTO: NATIONAL REPRODUCTIONS

Fig. 284   *General Electric Company*
Appliance Park-East, Air Conditioning Building
Sol King, F.A.I.A., and Albert Kahn Associates
Columbia, Maryland
PHOTO: NATIONAL REPRODUCTIONS

Fig. 285   *The Washington Post*
Newspaper Publishing Building, Additions and Alterations
Sol King, F.A.I.A., and Albert Kahn Associates
Washington, D.C.
PHOTO: NATIONAL REPRODUCTIONS

Fig. 286   *Ford Motor Company*
Service Parts Processing Redistribution Center
Brownstown Township, Michigan
PHOTO: NATIONAL REPRODUCTIONS

Fig. 287   *Fisher-New Center Company*
Office Building and Parking Structure
Detroit, Michigan
PHOTO: NATIONAL REPRODUCTIONS

Fig. 288   *Fisher-New Center Company*
Office Building
Detroit, Michigan
PHOTO: NATIONAL REPRODUCTIONS